AR & VR Development Mastery: Creating Immersive Experiences from Beginner to Expert

Kameron Hussain and Frahaan Hussain

Published by Sonar Publishing, 2025.

AR & VR DEVELOPMENT MASTERY: CREATING IMMERSIVE EXPERIENCES FROM BEGINNER TO EXPERT

First edition. April 6, 2025.

ISBN: 979-8230050728

Written by Kameron Hussain and Frahaan Hussain.

AR & VR Development Mastery

FIRST EDITION

CREATING IMMERSIVE EXPERIENCES FROM BEGINNER TO EXPERT

Preface

Augmented Reality (AR) and Virtual Reality (VR) have rapidly evolved from niche technologies into mainstream tools reshaping multiple industries. From immersive gaming experiences to life-saving applications in healthcare, the potential of AR and VR continues to expand. This book is designed to provide a comprehensive understanding of these technologies, from fundamental principles to advanced development techniques.

We begin with an **Introduction to AR & VR**, covering their history, evolution, and the critical distinctions between AR, VR, and Mixed Reality (MR). The first chapter also explores the transformative impact of these technologies across industries such as healthcare, education, retail, and more.

Next, we dive into the **Fundamentals of AR & VR Development**, detailing the necessary hardware, software, and programming tools required to create immersive experiences. Developers will gain insight into **3D graphics, spatial computing, and essential programming languages** used in AR and VR projects.

With a strong foundation in place, the book transitions into the **Building Blocks of AR & VR Experiences**, where we explore 3D modeling, user interface design, motion tracking, and techniques to optimize performance and reduce latency.

The following two chapters focus on **Developing AR & VR Applications**, with separate discussions on **Augmented Reality SDKs** (such as ARKit, ARCore, and Vuforia) and **Virtual Reality SDKs** (such as Oculus, SteamVR, and OpenXR). We cover topics such as **marker-based vs. markerless AR, object recognition,**

spatial mapping, immersive environment design, 6DOF movement, and best practices for minimizing motion sickness.

For those looking to push the boundaries of AR and VR development, the book presents **Advanced Techniques**, including **AI integration, cloud computing, networking, and rendering techniques for realism**.

A dedicated chapter explores **AR & VR in Gaming and Entertainment**, highlighting the role of game engines, narrative design, multiplayer experiences, and monetization strategies. Following this, we examine **business and enterprise applications**, showcasing how AR & VR revolutionize training, healthcare, real estate, and e-commerce.

Understanding **Testing, Debugging, and Deployment** is crucial for developers, and we provide in-depth guidance on **debugging tools, user feedback collection, deployment strategies, and project maintenance**.

As AR & VR continue to evolve, the book concludes with a **look into the future**, discussing upcoming **trends, ethical considerations, the role of AR & VR in the Metaverse, and how developers can prepare for the next wave of innovations.**

Table of Contents

Spatial Computing

Six Degrees of Freedom (6DOF)

Three Degrees of Freedom (3DOF)

Field of View (FoV)

Latency

Refresh Rate

Rendering Pipeline

Foveated Rendering

Depth Perception

Haptic Feedback

Inside-Out Tracking

Outside-In Tracking

Positional Tracking

Hand Tracking

Eye Tracking

Gaze-Based Interaction

Room-Scale VR

Passthrough AR

Light Field Display

SLAM (Simultaneous Localization and Mapping)

Object Occlusion

Occlusion Culling

Raycasting

World Anchors

Plane Detection

Marker-Based AR

Markerless AR

AR Cloud

Volumetric Capture

Photogrammetry

VR Locomotion

Comfort Mode

Room Setup

SDK (Software Development Kit)

OpenXR

WebXR

Metaverse

Persistent AR

XR Input System

Gesture Recognition

Chapter 1: Introduction to AR & VR

Understanding Augmented Reality (AR) and Virtual Reality (VR)

AUGMENTED REALITY (AR) and Virtual Reality (VR) are two of the most transformative technologies of the modern digital landscape. Both offer unique experiences that blend digital and physical worlds but operate in fundamentally different ways. In this section, we will explore what AR and VR are, their core principles, and how they are shaping the future of human-computer interaction.

What is Augmented Reality (AR)?

AUGMENTED REALITY OVERLAYS digital content onto the real world, enhancing the user's perception of their environment. Unlike VR, which immerses users in a completely virtual space, AR supplements reality by integrating digital elements into real-world settings.

Some of the most common implementations of AR include:

- **Mobile AR applications** – Apps like Pokémon GO and Snapchat filters use a smartphone's camera to overlay digital objects onto real-world scenes.

- **Smart glasses and headsets** – Devices such as Microsoft HoloLens and Magic Leap provide AR experiences by projecting holograms into the user's field of vision.

- **Industrial and enterprise applications** – AR is used in fields like manufacturing, medicine, and retail to provide real-time data visualization, remote assistance, and training simulations.

AR relies on various technologies, including **computer vision, depth tracking, and artificial intelligence** (**AI**) to recognize and enhance physical environments dynamically.

What is Virtual Reality (VR)?

VIRTUAL REALITY IS a fully immersive technology that transports users to a completely digital environment, blocking out the real world. VR environments are experienced through head-mounted displays (HMDs) and motion-tracking systems, creating an interactive virtual space.

Key components of VR include:

- **Head-mounted displays (HMDs)** – Devices such as the Oculus Quest, PlayStation VR, and HTC Vive provide an immersive, stereoscopic display that surrounds the user's vision.
- **Motion controllers and sensors** – VR systems track user movements using handheld controllers, gloves, or full-body tracking systems.
- **6 Degrees of Freedom (6DOF)** – Advanced VR setups allow users to move freely in a 3D space, enhancing realism.

VR is widely used in gaming, training simulations, virtual tourism, and collaborative workspaces, allowing users to engage with digital environments naturally.

Key Differences Between AR and VR

WHILE AR AND VR SHARE similarities in their use of 3D graphics and spatial computing, they differ in several critical ways:

Feature	Augmented Reality (AR)	Virtual Reality (VR)
Immersion	Partially immersive	Fully immersive
Hardware	Smartphones, tablets, smart glasses	VR headsets, motion controllers
User Interaction	Interacts with real-world elements	Interacts with a fully virtual world
Use Cases	Navigation, training, retail, gaming	Gaming, simulations, social VR, design

How AR & VR Are Transforming Industries

BOTH AR AND VR HAVE significant applications across various industries:

- **Healthcare:** AR assists in medical training, surgery guidance, and remote diagnostics, while VR is used for pain management, therapy, and medical simulations.
- **Education:** AR makes learning interactive with real-time overlays, while VR creates immersive historical reconstructions and laboratory simulations.
- **Retail and E-Commerce:** AR enables virtual try-ons for fashion and furniture, while VR allows users to experience virtual showrooms.
- **Real Estate:** Virtual home tours and AR property visualization streamline the buying process.

- **Manufacturing:** AR improves efficiency with real-time work instructions and remote collaboration.

- **Gaming and Entertainment:** VR revolutionizes gaming experiences with immersive worlds, while AR enhances mobile gaming and social media interactions.

The Convergence of AR and VR: Mixed Reality (MR)

MIXED REALITY (MR) blends elements of both AR and VR, allowing digital objects to interact with the real world in real-time. Devices like the **Microsoft HoloLens** and **Magic Leap** exemplify MR by enabling users to manipulate digital objects while maintaining awareness of their physical surroundings.

MR technology is advancing rapidly, with applications in **engineering, medical training, and collaborative workspaces**. By integrating AR and VR features, MR offers a flexible, hybrid approach to immersive experiences.

Conclusion

AUGMENTED REALITY AND Virtual Reality are reshaping the way we interact with digital content, offering new opportunities for businesses, developers, and consumers. As these technologies continue to evolve, their applications will expand, merging the physical and digital worlds in innovative ways.

The following sections will explore the historical evolution of AR and VR, the key technological advancements that have shaped them, and the role they play in the future of computing.

History and Evolution of AR & VR

THE JOURNEY OF AUGMENTED Reality (AR) and Virtual Reality (VR) is deeply rooted in the development of computer graphics, interactive media, and immersive technology. While both AR and VR have gained immense popularity in recent years, their origins date back several decades. Understanding the history of these technologies provides insight into their current capabilities and future potential.

Early Concepts and Theoretical Foundations

THE IDEA OF IMMERSIVE and augmented experiences has been envisioned long before the development of digital technology. Science fiction literature, films, and early theoretical research laid the foundation for what would later become AR and VR.

- **1838 - Stereoscopic Imaging:** Charles Wheatstone invented the **stereoscope**, which demonstrated that the human brain processes two slightly different images from each eye to create a sense of depth. This principle would later become essential in VR headset technology.

- **1935 - "Pygmalion's Spectacles":** Stanley G. Weinbaum published a science fiction short story envisioning a pair of goggles that could create an interactive, virtual experience with sight, sound, and even touch.

- **1950s - Morton Heilig's Sensorama:** A mechanical device that combined **stereoscopic 3D visuals, sound, vibration, and even scents** to create an immersive cinema-like experience. While not interactive, it was one of the first attempts at immersive virtual experiences.

The Birth of AR & VR Technology (1960s - 1980s)

THE FIRST REAL STEPS toward modern AR and VR systems began in the 1960s with pioneering research in computer graphics, head-mounted displays (HMDs), and interactive computing.

- **1968 - The First Head-Mounted Display:** Ivan Sutherland, a computer scientist, developed the "**Sword of Damocles,**" the first HMD. It displayed simple wireframe graphics and was too heavy to wear without being suspended from the ceiling.

- **1974 - Videoplace by Myron Krueger:** An early form of **interactive AR**, this system allowed users to interact with digital environments using body movement. It used projectors and cameras instead of headsets.

- **1982 - Aspen Movie Map:** Developed by MIT, this project was an early example of VR-like navigation, allowing users to explore a digital recreation of Aspen, Colorado, using pre-recorded video footage.

During this period, military and academic institutions started investing heavily in simulation technologies for pilot training, battlefield simulations, and remote operations.

The Rise of Consumer AR & VR (1990s - 2000s)

WITH ADVANCEMENTS IN computing power, commercial applications of AR and VR began emerging, although they were limited by **high costs and hardware limitations**.

- **1991 - Virtuality Arcade Machines:** One of the first **commercial VR gaming systems**, featuring **headsets and**

motion controllers. These machines allowed users to experience immersive 3D worlds, albeit with limited graphical fidelity.

- **1992 - The Birth of Augmented Reality:** Tom Caudell, a researcher at Boeing, coined the term "**Augmented Reality**" to describe digital overlays used in aircraft assembly.

- **1995 - Nintendo Virtual Boy:** A failed attempt at bringing VR gaming to consumers. The device provided a rudimentary 3D experience but suffered from **poor graphics, discomfort, and lack of software support**.

- **1999 - ARToolkit:** Hirokazu Kato developed **AR Toolkit**, an open-source AR software library that enabled marker-based AR applications using cameras and simple code.

By the early 2000s, AR started gaining momentum in industries like medicine, automotive, and entertainment, while VR continued to struggle due to **cost and motion sickness issues**.

Breakthroughs in Modern AR & VR (2010 - Present)

THE 2010S MARKED A major **resurgence of AR and VR** due to rapid advancements in mobile computing, cloud processing, and graphics technology.

- **2010 - Oculus Rift Prototype:** Palmer Luckey developed an early prototype of the **Oculus Rift**, which led to a VR revolution after its Kickstarter campaign raised millions in funding.

- **2013 - Google Glass:** A notable attempt at AR smart glasses. While it failed as a consumer product, it influenced AR development in industrial and medical applications.

- **2014 - Facebook Acquires Oculus:** Facebook's $2 billion acquisition of **Oculus VR** legitimized VR as a mainstream industry.

- **2015 - Microsoft HoloLens:** Introduced as the first **true Mixed Reality (MR) headset**, allowing users to interact with holograms in their physical environment.

- **2016 - Pokémon GO:** A cultural phenomenon that introduced **location-based AR gaming** to millions, demonstrating AR's potential in mainstream applications.

- **2019 - AR and VR in Enterprise:** Industries like retail, healthcare, and education started adopting AR and VR for **training, virtual meetings, and simulations.**

Technological Advancements in AR & VR

SEVERAL KEY ADVANCEMENTS have contributed to the rapid evolution of AR and VR:

1. Improved Display Technology

- **OLED and MicroLED displays** enable higher resolution and better contrast.

- **Higher refresh rates (90Hz - 120Hz)** reduce motion sickness in VR.

2. Advanced Motion Tracking and AI Integration

- **Inside-out tracking** allows VR headsets to track movement without external sensors.
- **AI-driven AR experiences** use machine learning to enhance object recognition.

3. Cloud and 5G Connectivity

- **Cloud-based AR & VR streaming** reduces hardware dependency.
- **5G enables real-time rendering and AR collaboration**.

4. Open Standards and SDKs

- **OpenXR and WebXR** provide cross-platform compatibility.
- **SDKs like ARKit, ARCore, and Vuforia** have democratized AR development.

Current Applications and Future Trends

TODAY, AR AND VR ARE reshaping industries in multiple ways:

Industry	AR Applications	VR Applications
Gaming	AR-enhanced mobile games (e.g., Pokémon GO)	Fully immersive VR games (e.g., Half-Life: Alyx)
Education	Interactive AR textbooks	Virtual classrooms and training
Healthcare	AR surgery guidance	VR therapy and pain management
Retail	Virtual try-on apps	VR shopping experiences
Real Estate	AR property visualization	VR home tours

The Future of AR & VR

THE NEXT DECADE PROMISES even **greater integration of AR and VR into everyday life**, with key trends including:

- **The Metaverse:** VR-driven social interactions and persistent digital worlds.
- **AR Smart Glasses:** Lightweight, always-on AR replacing smartphones.
- **AI and AR Convergence:** AI-enhanced AR for advanced object recognition.
- **Haptic Feedback and Neural Interfaces:** Full sensory immersion in VR.

Conclusion

FROM EARLY STEREOSCOPIC experiments to AI-powered AR and VR systems, the evolution of immersive technology has been marked by **continuous innovation and breakthroughs**. As hardware becomes more accessible and software capabilities expand, AR and VR will continue to **reshape how we interact with the digital and physical worlds.**

The next chapter will delve into **the fundamentals of AR & VR development**, exploring the hardware, software, and tools that make these immersive experiences possible.

Key Differences Between AR, VR, and Mixed Reality (MR)

AUGMENTED REALITY (AR), Virtual Reality (VR), and Mixed Reality (MR) are three distinct yet interconnected immersive technologies that are revolutionizing the way humans interact with digital environments. While they share similarities in their use of computer-generated content and real-time user interaction, their core functionalities, hardware requirements, and applications differ significantly. This section provides an in-depth comparison of AR, VR, and MR, highlighting their unique characteristics, use cases, and future potential.

Understanding Augmented Reality (AR)

AUGMENTED REALITY ENHANCES the real world by overlaying digital elements, such as images, text, sounds, and 3D objects, onto the user's physical environment. Unlike VR, AR does not replace reality but instead adds to it, providing an interactive experience where the real world and virtual objects coexist.

Core Features of AR

- **Overlay of Digital Content:** AR projects virtual objects onto the real-world environment.

- **Real-Time Interaction:** Users can engage with augmented elements dynamically.

- **Device Compatibility:** AR can be experienced through smartphones, tablets, AR smart glasses, and heads-up displays.

- **Marker-Based and Markerless AR:** AR applications can use visual markers (QR codes, printed images) or environment recognition for interaction.

Examples of AR Applications

1. **Gaming:** Pokémon GO and mobile AR games integrate virtual creatures into real-world locations.
2. **Retail and E-Commerce:** Virtual try-ons for fashion and home decor allow customers to visualize products before purchasing.
3. **Education:** AR-enhanced textbooks and interactive learning modules improve engagement in classrooms.
4. **Healthcare:** AR-assisted surgery provides real-time overlays of anatomical structures.
5. **Industrial Use:** AR is used for maintenance, remote assistance, and worker training in industries like manufacturing and automotive.

Simple Code Example: AR Object Placement with ARKit (Swift)

THE FOLLOWING EXAMPLE demonstrates placing a 3D object in an AR scene using **ARKit** in iOS:

```
import ARKit
```

```
import SceneKit
class ViewController: UIViewController, ARSCNViewDelegate {
@IBOutlet var sceneView: ARSCNView!
override func viewDidLoad() {
super.viewDidLoad()
sceneView.delegate = self
let sphere = SCNSphere(radius: 0.1)
let node = SCNNode(geometry: sphere)
node.position = SCNVector3(0, 0, -0.5)
sceneView.scene.rootNode.addChildNode(node)
}
override func viewWillAppear(_ animated: Bool) {
super.viewWillAppear(animated)
let configuration = ARWorldTrackingConfiguration()
sceneView.session.run(configuration)
}
override func viewWillDisappear(_ animated: Bool) {
super.viewWillDisappear(animated)
sceneView.session.pause()
}
```

```
}
```

This code initializes an AR session and places a **3D sphere** in the user's real-world environment.

Understanding Virtual Reality (VR)

VIRTUAL REALITY IMMERSES users in a fully digital environment, isolating them from the real world. Unlike AR, VR does not integrate physical surroundings but creates an entirely artificial space where users can interact with digital objects and navigate virtual worlds.

Core Features of VR

- **Fully Immersive Environment:** Users experience a complete digital environment with no visibility of the real world.
- **HMD and Motion Controllers:** VR is experienced through head-mounted displays (HMDs) like Oculus Rift, HTC Vive, and PlayStation VR.
- **6 Degrees of Freedom (6DOF):** Users can move freely in a virtual space and interact with objects.
- **Requires High Computational Power:** VR applications demand powerful GPUs for rendering real-time 3D environments.

Examples of VR Applications

1. **Gaming:** VR gaming allows users to interact with digital environments using natural movements.

2. **Training Simulations:** Pilots, military personnel, and medical professionals use VR simulations for practice.
3. **Architecture and Real Estate:** VR allows potential buyers to take virtual tours of properties.
4. **Therapy and Rehabilitation:** VR is used in exposure therapy for PTSD and in rehabilitation exercises for physical therapy.
5. **Social VR:** Platforms like VRChat and Meta's Horizon Worlds create shared social experiences in virtual spaces.

Simple Code Example: VR Interaction with Unity (C#)

THIS EXAMPLE SHOWS how to interact with VR objects in **Unity using the XR Toolkit**:

```
using UnityEngine;

using UnityEngine.XR.Interaction.Toolkit;

public class VRGrab : MonoBehaviour

{

public XRGrabInteractable interactable;

void Start()

{

interactable = GetComponent<XRGrabInteractable>();

interactable.onSelectEntered.AddListener(Grab);

}

void Grab(XRBaseInteractor interactor)
```

```
{
Debug.Log("Object grabbed by " + interactor.gameObject.name);
}
}
```

This script allows VR users to **pick up and interact with objects** using controllers.

Understanding Mixed Reality (MR)

MIXED REALITY IS AN advanced hybrid of AR and VR, where digital and physical objects interact in real-time. MR extends AR's capabilities by **anchoring virtual content in the real world** while allowing users to manipulate and interact with it dynamically.

Core Features of MR

- **Blends Real and Virtual Worlds:** MR creates a seamless integration of digital elements with real-world physics.
- **Interactive and Spatial Awareness:** MR applications use spatial computing to recognize and interact with surfaces, objects, and environments.
- **Device-Specific:** MR requires specialized headsets such as Microsoft HoloLens and Magic Leap.
- **Hand and Gesture Tracking:** Users can interact with digital content using hand gestures without needing controllers.

Examples of MR Applications

1. **Medical Training:** MR enables surgeons to visualize 3D holograms of organs during procedures.
2. **Industrial Design:** Engineers can create and manipulate 3D models in real-world environments.
3. **Collaborative Workspaces:** MR enables remote teams to collaborate in shared holographic spaces.
4. **Military and Defense:** MR is used in combat simulations and tactical planning.

Simple Code Example: Holographic Interaction in MR (HoloLens with MRTK)

THE FOLLOWING CODE demonstrates gesture-based interaction in an MR application using **Microsoft's Mixed Reality Toolkit (MRTK)**:

```
using Microsoft.MixedReality.Toolkit.Input;

using Microsoft.MixedReality.Toolkit.Utilities;

using UnityEngine;

public class MRObjectManipulation : MonoBehaviour, IMixedRealityPointerHandler

{

public void OnPointerDown(MixedRealityPointerEventData eventData)

{

Debug.Log("Object selected: " + gameObject.name);
```

```
}

public void OnPointerDragged(MixedRealityPointerEventData eventData) { }

public void OnPointerUp(MixedRealityPointerEventData eventData) { }

public void OnPointerClicked(MixedRealityPointerEventData eventData)

{

Debug.Log("Object clicked!");

}

}
```

This script enables **gesture-based selection and interaction with holograms** in MR applications.

Key Differences Between AR, VR, and MR

THE FOLLOWING TABLE summarizes the fundamental differences between AR, VR, and MR:

Feature	Augmented Reality (AR)	Virtual Reality (VR)	Mixed Reality (MR)
Immersion	Partial	Full	Hybrid
Environment	Real-world with overlays	Fully digital	Real + digital interactions
Devices	Smartphones, AR glasses	VR headsets	HoloLens, Magic Leap
Interaction	Touch, gaze, basic hand gestures	Motion controllers, 6DOF tracking	Hand gestures, voice, spatial tracking
Use Cases	Retail, healthcare, navigation	Gaming, training, social VR	Medical imaging, industrial design

Conclusion

AUGMENTED REALITY (AR), Virtual Reality (VR), and Mixed Reality (MR) each provide unique immersive experiences, catering to different industries and user needs. While AR enhances the real world with digital overlays, VR transports users to fully virtual spaces, and MR bridges the gap by allowing real and digital elements to interact. As technology advances, the lines between these immersive realities will continue to blur, unlocking new possibilities for **education, entertainment, business, and beyond**.

In the next section, we will explore the **impact of AR and VR on various industries**, examining how these technologies are transforming businesses and consumer experiences globally.

The Impact of AR & VR on Various Industries

AUGMENTED REALITY (AR) and Virtual Reality (VR) are transforming industries across the globe, revolutionizing how businesses operate, how consumers engage with products and services, and how professionals train for high-stakes roles. These technologies extend beyond entertainment and gaming, driving innovation in healthcare, education, retail, real estate, manufacturing, and more. As AR and VR continue to mature, their impact is expected to reshape the digital and physical worlds in unprecedented ways.

Healthcare: AR & VR in Medical Training, Surgery, and Therapy

AR AND VR ARE BEING widely adopted in the healthcare sector, improving medical training, surgical precision, and patient rehabilitation.

Medical Training & Simulation

MEDICAL PROFESSIONALS use VR simulations to practice complex procedures without the need for a live patient. VR medical training enables:

- **Anatomy visualization:** Medical students can explore interactive 3D models of the human body.
- **Surgical practice:** Surgeons can perform virtual procedures, improving accuracy before real operations.

- **Emergency response training:** VR environments simulate critical scenarios such as cardiac arrest or mass casualty incidents.

Example: VR Surgical Simulation

```
# EXAMPLE OF A VR SURGICAL training module using Unity
import UnityEngine
class SurgerySimulator:
def __init__(self):
self.instruments = ["scalpel", "forceps", "sutures"]
self.patient_condition = "stable"
def use_instrument(self, instrument):
if instrument in self.instruments:
print(f"Using {instrument} on virtual patient.")
else:
print("Instrument not available.")
surgery = SurgerySimulator()
surgery.use_instrument("scalpel")
```

This script represents a simplified VR simulation where medical trainees can interact with surgical instruments.

Augmented Reality in Surgery

AR IS USED TO OVERLAY real-time information onto a surgeon's field of vision, improving precision and reducing errors. **AR-assisted surgery** enhances procedures like:

- **Minimally invasive surgeries** where AR overlays anatomical structures for better navigation.
- **Neurosurgery** where AR visualizes brain tumors with high accuracy.
- **Orthopedic surgery** where AR aids in precise implant placements.

Therapeutic Applications

VR IS WIDELY USED IN therapy and rehabilitation for:

- **Mental health treatments:** VR exposure therapy is used for treating PTSD, phobias, and anxiety disorders.
- **Pain management:** VR distraction techniques help reduce pain perception during treatments.
- **Stroke rehabilitation:** Patients regain motor functions by performing VR-guided exercises.

Education and Training: AR & VR in Learning Environments

EDUCATION IS BEING revolutionized by AR and VR, making learning more **immersive, interactive, and engaging**.

Classroom Learning

- AR brings subjects like **history, geography, and science** to life with interactive 3D models.
- VR creates **historical reconstructions** where students can explore events like ancient civilizations.
- Virtual field trips enable students to visit **Mars, the Great Wall of China, or the human brain.**

Example: AR-Based Learning App

```
// EXAMPLE OF AN AR EDUCATIONAL app using JavaScript and WebAR

function loadARObject(modelURL) {

let scene = document.querySelector("a-scene");

let entity = document.createElement("a-entity");

entity.setAttribute("gltf-model", modelURL);

entity.setAttribute("position", "0 1 -3");

scene.appendChild(entity);

}

loadARObject("models/dinosaur.glb"); // Loads a 3D dinosaur model in AR
```

This JavaScript code adds a **3D dinosaur model** in an AR-based educational experience.

Workforce Training

AR & VR ARE USED TO train employees in industries like:

- **Manufacturing:** AR overlays guide workers in assembling complex machinery.
- **Retail:** VR retail training simulates customer service scenarios.
- **Military & Defense:** VR combat training enhances situational awareness.

Retail & E-Commerce: AR & VR in Shopping Experiences

RETAILERS ARE INTEGRATING AR and VR to **enhance customer experience, reduce returns, and increase sales.**

Augmented Reality in Shopping

- **Virtual try-ons:** AR allows customers to see how clothes, makeup, and accessories look on them.
- **Furniture placement:** Apps like **IKEA Place** use AR to let users preview furniture in their homes.
- **AR-enabled packaging:** Brands use AR for interactive product experiences.

Virtual Reality in Retail

- **VR stores:** Customers browse virtual malls from home.

- **VR product demonstrations:** Brands showcase products in an interactive VR environment.

Example: AR Virtual Try-On (Python with OpenCV)

```
IMPORT CV2

def apply_virtual_glasses(image_path):

image = cv2.imread(image_path)

overlay = cv2.imread("glasses.png", cv2.IMREAD_UNCHANGED)

x_offset, y_offset = 100, 100 # Position of glasses overlay

image[y_offset:y_offset+overlay.shape[0], x_offset:x_offset+overlay.shape[1]] = overlay

cv2.imshow("Virtual Try-On", image)

cv2.waitKey(0)

apply_virtual_glasses("user_face.jpg")
```

This script simulates **AR-based virtual glasses try-on** using OpenCV.

Real Estate & Architecture: AR & VR in Property Visualization

AR AND VR REVOLUTIONIZE **how buyers, architects, and interior designers** interact with properties.

Virtual Reality for Real Estate

- Buyers explore **3D virtual home tours** before visiting a physical location.
- Architects create **walkable VR simulations** of new buildings.

Augmented Reality in Real Estate

- AR overlays **blueprints onto construction sites** for better project visualization.
- Homebuyers use **AR apps to visualize home improvements.**

Manufacturing & Engineering: AR & VR in Product Development

AR AND VR **streamline industrial operations, reduce costs, and improve efficiency**.

Augmented Reality in Manufacturing

- **AR work instructions:** Digital overlays guide factory workers in complex tasks.
- **Remote assistance:** Technicians receive **real-time AR instructions** from experts.

Virtual Reality in Engineering

- **VR prototyping:** Engineers design and test machinery in VR before production.
- **Digital twins:** Factories create **VR replicas** of machinery for maintenance.

Entertainment & Media: AR & VR in Film, TV, and Gaming

THE **entertainment industry** has been one of the biggest adopters of AR and VR.

AR in Media & Advertising

- AR ads create **interactive billboards and holographic displays.**
- AR-powered apps like **Snapchat and Instagram filters** enhance social media engagement.

VR in Film & Gaming

- VR enables **360-degree storytelling** in films.
- Gaming platforms like **Oculus Quest and PlayStation VR** deliver full-immersion experiences.

Example: VR Game Character Movement (C# in Unity)

USING UNITYENGINE;

```
public class VRMovement : MonoBehaviour

{

public float speed = 2.0f;

void Update()

{

float moveX = Input.GetAxis("Horizontal") * speed * Time.deltaTime;

float moveZ = Input.GetAxis("Vertical") * speed * Time.deltaTime;

transform.Translate(moveX, 0, moveZ);

}

}
```

This script controls **VR player movement** in a virtual environment.

Conclusion

AR AND VR ARE RESHAPING industries by **enhancing experiences, improving training, reducing costs, and unlocking new business opportunities**. Whether it's **saving lives in healthcare, revolutionizing retail, or transforming real estate**, the adoption of immersive technologies will continue to **accelerate digital transformation across sectors**.

In the next chapter, we will explore the **fundamentals of AR and VR development**, examining the hardware, software, and platforms used to create these groundbreaking experiences.

Chapter 2: Fundamentals of AR & VR Development

Overview of AR & VR Hardware and Devices

AUGMENTED REALITY (AR) and Virtual Reality (VR) rely on specialized hardware to create immersive and interactive experiences. Understanding the different types of AR and VR hardware is essential for developers, as it impacts the design, functionality, and overall feasibility of applications. This section explores the fundamental components of AR and VR hardware, including head-mounted displays (HMDs), tracking devices, input methods, and computing power requirements.

1. AR & VR Head-Mounted Displays (HMDs)

HMDS ARE THE MOST CRITICAL hardware components for both AR and VR experiences. They serve as the primary display devices, providing users with digital content superimposed on the real world (AR) or fully immersive environments (VR). These can be categorized as follows:

AR Headsets

- **Microsoft HoloLens (HoloLens 2)**: A standalone AR headset with spatial mapping, gesture recognition, and enterprise-focused applications.
- **Magic Leap 2**: A lightweight AR headset that leverages spatial computing and mixed reality.

- **Epson Moverio**: A transparent display headset mainly used for industrial applications.

- **Nreal Light & Nreal Air**: Consumer-oriented AR glasses that connect to mobile devices for lightweight AR experiences.

VR Headsets

- **Meta Quest Series (Quest 2, Quest 3, Quest Pro)**: Standalone VR headsets with built-in computing power, capable of inside-out tracking.

- **HTC Vive Series (Vive Pro, Vive XR Elite, Vive Focus 3)**: Premium VR headsets designed for gaming and enterprise use, featuring high-resolution displays and advanced tracking.

- **Valve Index**: A high-end VR headset for PC-based experiences, known for its precise tracking and high refresh rate.

- **Sony PlayStation VR2**: A console-based VR headset designed for the PlayStation 5.

EACH HMD VARIES IN its display technology, field of view (FoV), refresh rate, and resolution, impacting the user's overall experience.

2. Tracking and Motion Sensors

TRACKING IS A CRUCIAL aspect of AR & VR, as it determines how well the system understands the user's position and movements within an environment. Various tracking technologies include:

Inside-Out Tracking

INSIDE-OUT TRACKING utilizes onboard cameras and sensors to map the environment and track the user's movement without external hardware. Popular implementations include:

- **Oculus Insight (Meta Quest)**
- **Microsoft HoloLens SLAM (Simultaneous Localization and Mapping)**
- **Lighthouse-Free Vive Focus 3 Tracking**

Outside-In Tracking

OUTSIDE-IN TRACKING requires external sensors or base stations to track the user's movement with high accuracy. Examples include:

- **Valve Lighthouse Tracking (Valve Index, HTC Vive)**
- **OptiTrack and Vicon (Enterprise-Level Motion Tracking Systems)**

Hand and Eye Tracking

MODERN AR AND VR SYSTEMS incorporate additional tracking capabilities, such as:

- **Hand Tracking**: Enables gesture-based interaction (e.g., HoloLens 2, Quest 2).

- **Eye Tracking**: Enhances realism and improves rendering efficiency by focusing graphical power where the user is looking (e.g., PlayStation VR2, Varjo XR-3).

3. Input Devices and Controllers

INTERACTION IN AR & VR environments requires specialized input devices, including:

VR Controllers

VR CONTROLLERS ALLOW precise interaction with virtual objects and environments. They often feature haptic feedback, buttons, triggers, and analog sticks.

- **Oculus Touch Controllers**: Used in Quest headsets, providing 6DoF tracking.

- **Valve Index Controllers (Knuckles Controllers)**: Feature individual finger tracking.

- **HTC Vive Controllers**: Used with Vive headsets for motion input.

Hand and Finger Tracking

SOME AR AND VR SYSTEMS allow direct interaction without controllers by tracking hand and finger movements.

- **Leap Motion Controller**: A peripheral device for finger tracking.

- **HoloLens 2 Hand Tracking**: Uses depth sensors for natural hand gestures.

Brain-Computer Interfaces (BCI) and Experimental Inputs

EMERGING TECHNOLOGIES like brain-computer interfaces (BCI) and electromyography (EMG) are being explored for controlling AR and VR experiences without traditional input devices.

4. Processing Units and Performance Considerations

AR & VR APPLICATIONS demand significant computing power to render high-quality graphics and maintain smooth performance. Hardware choices affect:

- **Latency**: The delay between user movement and system response should be minimized (<20ms for VR).
- **Frame Rate**: Most VR experiences target 90Hz or higher to prevent motion sickness.
- **Resolution**: Higher resolutions reduce screen-door effects but require better hardware.

Standalone vs. Tethered Devices

- **Standalone Headsets**: Contain built-in processors (e.g., Meta Quest 3, HoloLens 2).
- **PC-Connected VR**: Requires external powerful computers (e.g., Valve Index, HTC Vive Pro).
- **Mobile AR**: Uses smartphones or tablets for processing (e.g., ARKit, ARCore).

5. AR & VR Audio Systems

SPATIAL AUDIO ENHANCES immersion by simulating 3D soundscapes. Key technologies include:

- **Ambisonic Audio**: Used in VR to create a realistic sound environment.
- **HRTF (Head-Related Transfer Function)**: Helps replicate how sound naturally reaches the ears.
- **Binaural Audio**: Creates directional audio for VR headsets.

Many AR & VR headsets have built-in spatial audio support, while external devices like the **Oculus Earphones**, **Sony Pulse 3D Headset**, and **Valve Index Off-Ear Speakers** improve the experience.

6. Network Connectivity for AR & VR

NETWORK CONNECTIVITY is vital for multi-user AR & VR experiences, remote rendering, and cloud processing. Different use cases require:

- **5G & Edge Computing**: Low-latency streaming of AR/VR content.
- **Wi-Fi 6 & 6E**: Faster data transfer for standalone VR headsets.
- **Cloud VR**: Services like NVIDIA CloudXR allow cloud-based rendering.

7. Best Practices for Choosing AR & VR Hardware

WHEN SELECTING HARDWARE for an AR or VR project, developers should consider:

- **Target Audience**: Is it for consumers, enterprises, or industrial applications?
- **Performance Needs**: Does the application require high-end PC power or standalone processing?
- **Budget Constraints**: Cost differences between high-end headsets and entry-level solutions.
- **Interaction Style**: Does the project benefit more from controllers, hand tracking, or eye tracking?

8. Sample Code for Hardware Detection in Unity

FOR DEVELOPERS WORKING in **Unity**, identifying the connected AR/VR hardware dynamically is essential. Below is a sample C# script for detecting VR hardware:

```
using UnityEngine;

using UnityEngine.XR;

public class VRHardwareDetector : MonoBehaviour

{

void Start()

{

if (XRSettings.isDeviceActive)
```

```
{
Debug.Log("Active VR Device: " + XRSettings.loadedDeviceName);
Debug.Log("Eye Texture Resolution: " + XRSettings.eyeTextureWidth + " x " + XRSettings.eyeTextureHeight);
}
else
{
Debug.Log("No VR device detected.");
}
}
}
```

For **AR hardware detection**, Unity's **AR Foundation** package can be used:

```
using UnityEngine.XR.ARFoundation;
using UnityEngine.XR.ARSubsystems;
public class ARHardwareDetector : MonoBehaviour
{
ARSession session;
void Start()
{
```

```
session = GetComponent<ARSession>();
if (session.subsystem != null && session.subsystem.running)
{
Debug.Log("AR Hardware Detected: " + session.subsystem.subsystemDescriptor.id);
}
else
{
Debug.Log("No AR hardware detected.");
}
}
}
```

Conclusion

UNDERSTANDING AR & VR hardware is fundamental to developing optimized, immersive experiences. From HMDs and input devices to tracking systems and network connectivity, selecting the right hardware plays a crucial role in the success of AR & VR applications. Future advancements in AI-powered tracking, brain-computer interfaces, and cloud-based rendering will further revolutionize AR & VR hardware, making it more accessible and powerful.

Software and Platforms for AR & VR Development

DEVELOPING AR AND VR applications requires a combination of software tools, development platforms, and frameworks tailored for immersive experiences. These software solutions help developers create, test, and deploy AR/VR applications efficiently. In this section, we will explore the leading development environments, SDKs, APIs, and supporting tools used in AR and VR development.

1. Game Engines for AR & VR Development

GAME ENGINES PROVIDE the foundation for AR and VR applications by offering a set of tools for rendering, physics, input handling, and asset management. The two most commonly used engines for AR and VR are **Unity** and **Unreal Engine**.

Unity

UNITY IS A WIDELY USED game engine that supports both AR and VR development. Its advantages include:

- **Cross-platform support** (ARKit, ARCore, Oculus, SteamVR, OpenXR).
- **C# scripting** for easy development.
- **Extensive asset store** with AR/VR resources.
- **Strong community support** and documentation.

Unity provides built-in support for VR through **XR Interaction Toolkit** and for AR through **AR Foundation**, a framework that supports both **ARKit** (iOS) and **ARCore** (Android).

Unreal Engine

UNREAL ENGINE, DEVELOPED by Epic Games, is known for its high-fidelity rendering and robust VR support. Its advantages include:

- **Realistic graphics** with real-time ray tracing.
- **Blueprint visual scripting**, reducing the need for coding.
- **Built-in VR template** for quick prototyping.
- **C++ support** for custom development.

Unreal Engine is often used for **high-end VR applications**, such as simulations, training, and photorealistic experiences.

2. AR Development Frameworks and SDKs

AUGMENTED REALITY DEVELOPMENT requires specific SDKs that provide tracking, scene understanding, and interaction capabilities. The most popular AR development frameworks include:

ARKit (Apple)

ARKIT IS APPLE'S AR development framework for iOS, providing:

- **World tracking and plane detection**.
- **Object and image recognition**.
- **LiDAR support** for depth mapping.

- **Face tracking** for AR filters.

Example of initializing an ARKit session in Swift:

```
import ARKit

import SceneKit

let arView = ARSCNView(frame: UIScreen.main.bounds)

let configuration = ARWorldTrackingConfiguration()

configuration.planeDetection = .horizontal

arView.session.run(configuration)
```

ARCore (Google)

ARCORE IS GOOGLE'S AR SDK for Android and supports:

- **Motion tracking** using the phone's camera and sensors.
- **Light estimation** for realistic rendering.
- **Augmented Images** for recognizing and placing AR content.
- **Cloud Anchors** for multi-user AR experiences.

Example of creating an AR scene in ARCore:

```
Session session = new Session(context);

Config config = new Config(session);

config.setUpdateMode(Config.UpdateMode.LATEST_CAMERA_IMAG

session.configure(config);
```

Vuforia

VUFORIA IS A WIDELY used **marker-based AR** SDK that enables:

- **Image and object recognition.**
- **Cloud-based recognition.**
- **Model targets** for detecting 3D objects.
- **Integration with Unity.**

3. VR Development Frameworks and SDKs

VR DEVELOPMENT PLATFORMS provide tools for rendering immersive environments, handling input from VR controllers, and optimizing performance.

Oculus SDK

META (FORMERLY FACEBOOK) provides the **Oculus SDK**, which supports:

- **Oculus Quest and Rift headsets.**
- **Hand tracking and controller input.**
- **Spatial audio integration.**
- **Asynchronous SpaceWarp (ASW) for performance optimization.**

Unity example for Oculus integration:

```
using UnityEngine;
```

```
using Oculus.Platform;
using Oculus.Platform.Models;
void Start()
{
Core.Initialize();
Debug.Log("Oculus SDK Initialized");
}
```

SteamVR SDK

STEAMVR IS USED FOR VR applications on **Valve Index, HTC Vive, and other PC VR headsets**. It provides:

- **Lighthouse tracking support.**
- **Advanced input handling for controllers.**
- **Room-scale VR capabilities.**

Unity example for SteamVR input handling:

```
using UnityEngine;
using Valve.VR;
public class VRInput : MonoBehaviour
{
public SteamVR_Action_Boolean grabAction;
void Update()
```

```
{
if (grabAction.GetStateDown(SteamVR_Input_Sources.Any))
{
Debug.Log("Grab action detected!");
}
}
}
```

OpenXR

OPENXR IS AN OPEN STANDARD developed by **Khronos Group** that enables cross-platform VR development. It provides:

- **A unified API for VR hardware.**
- **Cross-device compatibility.**
- **Better long-term support for VR development.**

Example of OpenXR initialization in C++:

```
#include <openxr/openxr.h>

XrInstance instance;

XrInstanceCreateInfo createInfo = { XR_TYPE_INSTANCE_CREATE_INFO };

xrCreateInstance(&createInfo, &instance);
```

4. Supporting Tools for AR & VR Development

IN ADDITION TO GAME engines and SDKs, AR/VR development benefits from various supporting tools.

3D Modeling and Animation Tools

- **Blender** (Open-source 3D modeling software).
- **Autodesk Maya** (Industry-standard for high-end 3D animation).
- **ZBrush** (Used for sculpting detailed 3D models).

Spatial Mapping and Environment Scanning

- **Microsoft Azure Kinect** (3D scanning for AR applications).
- **LiDAR Sensors** (Used in iPhone Pro models for depth mapping).

Performance Optimization Tools

- **NVIDIA VRWorks** (Optimizes VR performance on NVIDIA GPUs).
- **AMD LiquidVR** (Optimizes VR applications for AMD GPUs).
- **Unity Profiler and Unreal Engine Insights** (Performance debugging tools).

5. Cloud Services for AR & VR

CLOUD COMPUTING ENHANCES AR and VR applications by enabling large-scale processing, multiplayer experiences, and persistent AR content.

Cloud Anchors

USED FOR **shared AR experiences** across multiple devices.

- **Google Cloud Anchors** (ARCore).
- **Apple ARKit Cloud Anchors.**

Streaming VR Experiences

- **NVIDIA CloudXR** (Cloud-based VR rendering).
- **Google Stadia and Meta's cloud VR experiments.**

AI and Machine Learning Integration

AI ENHANCES AR AND VR applications through:

- **Computer vision for object recognition.**
- **Speech recognition for VR assistants.**
- **Gesture tracking for controller-free interaction.**

6. Cross-Platform AR & VR Development Considerations

WHEN DEVELOPING AR & VR applications for multiple platforms, developers must consider:

- **Hardware limitations** (PC VR vs. standalone VR).
- **Performance trade-offs** (Higher fidelity vs. better frame rates).
- **Interaction differences** (Touch-based AR vs. controller-based VR).

Cross-Platform AR & VR Development Tools

- **Unity's XR Plugin Management** (Supports multiple VR devices).
- **AR Foundation (Unity)** (Supports both ARKit and ARCore).
- **WebXR** (Browser-based AR & VR).

7. Sample Project: Cross-Platform AR App in Unity

BELOW IS A SIMPLE UNITY script that initializes an AR session using AR Foundation:

```
using UnityEngine;

using UnityEngine.XR.ARFoundation;

using UnityEngine.XR.ARSubsystems;

public class ARManager : MonoBehaviour

{

private ARSession session;

void Start()
```

```
{
session = GetComponent<ARSession>();
if (session != null)
{
session.enabled = true;
Debug.Log("AR session started");
}
}
}
```

Conclusion

CHOOSING THE RIGHT software and platform for AR & VR development depends on factors such as **target audience, hardware support, and performance needs**. Developers must familiarize themselves with **game engines, SDKs, cloud services, and optimization tools** to create **immersive and high-performance AR/VR applications**. As the field continues to evolve, new platforms and tools will further enhance the development experience, making AR & VR more accessible and powerful across industries.

Key Programming Languages and Tools

DEVELOPING AR AND VR applications requires knowledge of various programming languages and development tools. These languages and tools enable developers to create immersive experiences, interact with 3D environments, handle real-time rendering, and integrate AR/VR-specific functionalities such as motion tracking, spatial mapping, and physics simulations.

This section explores the most commonly used programming languages for AR and VR development, the tools that facilitate the development process, and code examples illustrating their use.

1. Programming Languages for AR & VR Development

SEVERAL PROGRAMMING languages are commonly used in AR and VR development, each suited to different platforms, engines, and hardware requirements.

C#

C# IS THE PRIMARY LANGUAGE for Unity-based AR and VR development. It offers:

- Strong **integration with Unity**.
- Object-oriented programming with **garbage collection.**
- Extensive libraries for **game and app development**.

Example: Basic C# script for Unity to control an object in VR:

```
using UnityEngine;

public class RotateObject : MonoBehaviour

{

public float rotationSpeed = 50.0f;
```

```
void Update()
{
transform.Rotate(Vector3.up * rotationSpeed * Time.deltaTime);
}
}
```

C++

C++ IS WIDELY USED in **Unreal Engine** for high-performance AR and VR applications. It provides:

- **Lower-level access to hardware** for optimized performance.
- **Memory management control**, reducing latency.
- **Native integration** with Unreal Engine.

Example: C++ class in Unreal Engine controlling VR interactions:

```
#include "VRCharacter.h"
#include "GameFramework/Actor.h"
void AVRCharacter::MoveForward(float Value)
{
AddMovementInput(GetActorForwardVector(), Value);
}
```

Java

JAVA IS PRIMARILY USED for **Android-based AR applications**, particularly with **ARCore**.

Example: Setting up an ARCore session in Java:

```
Session session = new Session(context);

Config config = new Config(session);

config.setUpdateMode(Config.UpdateMode.LATEST_CAMERA_IMA(

session.configure(config);
```

Swift

SWIFT IS USED FOR **ARKit** development on iOS, allowing easy integration with Apple's ecosystem.

Example: Initializing an ARKit session in Swift:

```
import ARKit

let arView = ARSCNView(frame: UIScreen.main.bounds)

let configuration = ARWorldTrackingConfiguration()

arView.session.run(configuration)
```

Python

PYTHON IS NOT TYPICALLY used for **real-time AR/VR development**, but it is valuable for:

- **Prototyping**

- **Machine Learning integration**
- **Data analysis in AR applications**

Example: Using OpenCV for AR-based face detection:

```
import cv2

face_cascade = cv2.CascadeClassifier('haarcascade_frontalface_default.xml')

img = cv2.imread('face.jpg')

faces = face_cascade.detectMultiScale(img, 1.3, 5)

for (x,y,w,h) in faces:

cv2.rectangle(img, (x,y), (x+w, y+h), (255,0,0), 2)
```

2. Development Environments and IDEs

CHOOSING THE RIGHT Integrated Development Environment (IDE) is crucial for efficiency. Popular IDEs for AR/VR development include:

Unity Editor

- Best for **cross-platform AR/VR applications.**
- Supports **C# scripting.**
- **AR Foundation for ARKit and ARCore** integration.
- VR support via **XR Interaction Toolkit.**

Unreal Engine Editor

- High-performance rendering with **C++ and Blueprints**.
- Optimized for **photorealistic VR applications**.
- Native **OpenXR** and **SteamVR support**.

Android Studio

- Used for developing **ARCore applications** in Java/ Kotlin.
- Provides **AR scene debugging tools**.

Xcode

- Required for developing **ARKit applications**.
- Supports **Swift and Objective-C**.
- Built-in **SceneKit for 3D rendering**.

3. Frameworks and APIs for AR & VR Development

AR AND VR APPLICATIONS require specific **frameworks** and **APIs** to handle features like spatial tracking, physics simulation, and object rendering.

OpenXR

OPENXR IS AN OPEN STANDARD for **VR development** that allows applications to work across multiple VR hardware.

Example: Initializing an OpenXR instance in C++:

```
#include <openxr/openxr.h>

XrInstance instance;

XrInstanceCreateInfo createInfo = { XR_TYPE_INSTANCE_CREATE_INFO };

xrCreateInstance(&createInfo, &instance);
```

WebXR

WEBXR ALLOWS DEVELOPERS to create **browser-based AR and VR experiences.**

Example: Basic WebXR VR setup in JavaScript:

```
navigator.xr.requestSession('immersive-vr').then((session) => {

console.log("VR Session started");

});
```

4. Libraries and Toolkits for AR & VR Development

AR AND VR APPLICATIONS often rely on additional **libraries** and **toolkits** for enhanced functionality.

Three.js (Web-based 3D Rendering)

THREE.JS IS A JAVASCRIPT library that simplifies **3D rendering in the browser.**

Example: Creating a VR scene with Three.js:

```
const scene = new THREE.Scene();
```

```
const camera = new THREE.PerspectiveCamera(75, window.innerWidth / window.innerHeight, 0.1, 1000);

const renderer = new THREE.WebGLRenderer();

renderer.setSize(window.innerWidth, window.innerHeight);

document.body.appendChild(renderer.domElement);
```

Vuforia (AR Marker-Based Tracking)

VUFORIA IS AN AR SDK specializing in **marker-based AR** applications.

Oculus SDK (VR Development)

THE OCULUS SDK PROVIDES APIs for **VR development on Quest and Rift**.

SteamVR SDK (PC-based VR)

USED FOR DEVELOPING VR applications on **HTC Vive and Valve Index**.

5. Sample Project: VR Object Interaction in Unity

BELOW IS A UNITY C# script that allows VR users to pick up and interact with objects:

```
using UnityEngine;

using UnityEngine.XR.Interaction.Toolkit;

public class PickUpObject : XRGrabInteractable
```

```
{
protected override void OnSelectEntered(XRBaseInteractor interactor)
{
base.OnSelectEntered(interactor);
Debug.Log("Object Picked Up!");
}
}
```

6. Future Trends in AR & VR Programming

THE FUTURE OF AR & VR programming is evolving with advancements in:

- **AI integration** for object recognition and intelligent interactions.
- **Cloud-based AR** for persistent experiences.
- **5G and Edge Computing** to reduce latency in AR applications.
- **Haptic feedback and BCI (Brain-Computer Interfaces)** for advanced interaction.

Conclusion

CHOOSING THE RIGHT programming language and tools is essential for successful AR & VR development. While **C# and C++ dominate AR/VR applications**, web-based solutions like **WebXR** are expanding the possibilities. Frameworks like **OpenXR, ARKit,**

ARCore, and SteamVR SDKs allow seamless development across platforms. The continuous evolution of **AI, cloud computing, and 5G** will further enhance the future of AR and VR applications, making them more accessible and interactive across industries.

Understanding 3D Graphics and Spatial Computing

3D GRAPHICS AND SPATIAL computing form the foundation of AR and VR applications, enabling developers to create immersive digital experiences. Understanding how 3D graphics work, along with the principles of spatial computing, is essential for creating realistic, interactive, and efficient AR/VR applications. This section explores 3D rendering, coordinate systems, lighting, shaders, physics, and spatial computing techniques.

1. Fundamentals of 3D Graphics

3D GRAPHICS INVOLVE rendering objects in a three-dimensional space using mathematical models, textures, and lighting. Key components of 3D graphics include:

Vertices and Meshes

- A **vertex** is a point in 3D space, defined by its **x, y, and z coordinates.**
- A **mesh** is a collection of vertices connected to form polygons, usually triangles or quads.

EXAMPLE OF DEFINING a 3D cube in OpenGL:

```
float vertices[] = {
```

```
-0.5f, -0.5f, -0.5f,
0.5f, -0.5f, -0.5f,
0.5f, 0.5f, -0.5f,
-0.5f, 0.5f, -0.5f,
-0.5f, -0.5f, 0.5f,
0.5f, -0.5f, 0.5f,
0.5f, 0.5f, 0.5f,
-0.5f, 0.5f, 0.5f
};
```

Coordinate Systems

- **World Space**: The absolute position of objects in the 3D world.
- **Object Space**: The local coordinate system relative to an object's origin.
- **Camera Space**: The transformed space where objects are viewed from the camera's perspective.
- **Screen Space**: The final 2D representation of the 3D scene on the display.

Transformations

TRANSFORMATIONS MANIPULATE objects in 3D space using:

- **Translation** (Moving an object along x, y, or z).
- **Rotation** (Rotating around an axis).
- **Scaling** (Changing an object's size).

Example of rotating an object in Unity:

```
void Update() {
transform.Rotate(Vector3.up * Time.deltaTime * 50);
}
```

2. Rendering Pipeline in 3D Graphics

THE RENDERING PIPELINE processes 3D models into 2D images displayed on the screen. The main stages include:

1. Vertex Processing

EACH VERTEX IS TRANSFORMED from object space to world space, then to screen space.

2. Rasterization

CONVERTS 3D SHAPES into 2D pixels, determining visibility and color.

3. Fragment Processing

SHADING, LIGHTING, and texture mapping are applied.

4. Output to Screen

FINAL PIXELS ARE DISPLAYED, creating the rendered image.

3. Lighting and Shading in AR/VR

LIGHTING ENHANCES REALISM in 3D environments by simulating how light interacts with surfaces.

Types of Lighting

- **Ambient Light**: General background light.
- **Directional Light**: Simulates the sun, affecting all objects uniformly.
- **Point Light**: A light source emitting in all directions (e.g., a lamp).
- **Spotlight**: A focused light with an adjustable cone.
- **Area Light**: A broad, diffuse light source.

EXAMPLE OF ADDING A directional light in Unity:

```
Light dirLight = new GameObject("Directional Light").AddComponent<Light>();

dirLight.type = LightType.Directional;

dirLight.color = Color.white;
```

Shading Models

SHADING MODELS DEFINE how surfaces react to light.

- **Flat Shading**: Applies uniform color to each polygon.
- **Gouraud Shading**: Interpolates colors across vertices.
- **Phong Shading**: Interpolates normals for smoother lighting effects.
- **Physically Based Rendering (PBR)**: Simulates real-world materials.

4. Materials and Textures

TEXTURES ENHANCE VISUAL detail by applying images to 3D surfaces.

Texture Mapping

- **Diffuse Map**: Base color texture.
- **Normal Map**: Adds surface detail by simulating small bumps.
- **Specular Map**: Controls how shiny an object appears.
- **Emission Map**: Makes surfaces appear self-lit.

EXAMPLE OF APPLYING a texture in Unity:

```
Renderer rend = GetComponent<Renderer>();

rend.material.mainTexture = Resources.Load<Texture2D>("myTexture");
```

5. Physics in AR & VR

PHYSICS SIMULATIONS improve realism by enabling dynamic interactions. Key physics concepts include:

Rigid Body Dynamics

SIMULATES SOLID OBJECT motion.

Example in Unity:

```
Rigidbody rb = gameObject.AddComponent<Rigidbody>();

rb.mass = 5f;
```

Collisions and Triggers

DETECT WHEN OBJECTS touch or interact.

Example:

```
void OnCollisionEnter(Collision collision) {

Debug.Log("Collision detected with " + collision.gameObject.name);

}
```

6. Spatial Computing in AR & VR

SPATIAL COMPUTING INTEGRATES digital objects into the real world using sensors, AI, and computer vision.

1. Scene Understanding

- **Plane detection** (detecting floors, walls).
- **Depth perception** (LiDAR sensors enhance AR accuracy).
- **Object recognition** (identifying physical objects).

EXAMPLE OF PLANE DETECTION in ARKit:

```
let config = ARWorldTrackingConfiguration()

config.planeDetection = .horizontal

arView.session.run(config)
```

2. Spatial Mapping

SPATIAL MAPPING CREATES a digital representation of the real world.

Example of spatial mapping in Microsoft HoloLens:

```
SpatialMappingRenderer spatialMapping = new GameObject().AddComponent<SpatialMappingRenderer>();

spatialMapping.renderState = SpatialMappingRenderer.RenderState.Visualization;
```

3. Gesture and Motion Tracking

- **Hand tracking** (Quest 2, HoloLens).
- **Eye tracking** (PlayStation VR2).
- **Body tracking** (Kinect-style AR experiences).

7. Performance Optimization in 3D Graphics

Level of Detail (LOD)

SWITCHING BETWEEN HIGH and low-poly models based on distance improves performance.

Occlusion Culling

HIDES OBJECTS THAT are not visible to the camera.

Example:

```
Camera.main.cullingMask = 1 << LayerMask.NameToLayer("VisibleObjects");
```

Frame Rate Optimization

VR APPLICATIONS SHOULD run at **90Hz or higher** to prevent motion sickness.

Conclusion

UNDERSTANDING 3D GRAPHICS and spatial computing is crucial for AR and VR development. By leveraging rendering techniques, physics simulations, lighting models, and spatial mapping, developers can create immersive and efficient AR/VR applications. As technology advances, spatial computing will play a key role in defining next-generation digital experiences.

Chapter 3: Building Blocks of AR & VR Experiences

3D Modeling and Asset Creation for AR & VR

CREATING IMMERSIVE Augmented Reality (AR) and Virtual Reality (VR) experiences requires high-quality 3D models and assets. In AR and VR, digital objects must appear realistic, interact naturally with users, and maintain performance across different hardware configurations. This section explores the fundamentals of 3D modeling, asset optimization, and the best tools for developing assets in AR and VR environments.

Understanding 3D Modeling for AR & VR

3D MODELING IS THE process of creating three-dimensional representations of objects using specialized software. In AR and VR, 3D models serve as the foundation of digital environments and interactive elements. These models can range from simple geometric shapes to highly detailed characters and landscapes.

Key Aspects of 3D Modeling

1. **Polygon Count and Optimization**

○ AR and VR applications must balance visual fidelity and performance.

○ Models with high polygon counts (high-poly) offer detailed visuals but may cause performance issues.

○ Low-polygon (low-poly) models optimize performance while maintaining essential details.

○ Techniques such as normal mapping can add detail without increasing the polygon count.

2. **Texturing and Materials**

○ Textures enhance the realism of models by adding color, patterns, and surface details.

○ Common texture formats include PNG, JPG, and TGA.

○ Physically Based Rendering (PBR) materials simulate realistic lighting effects, such as reflections and shadows.

3. **UV Mapping**

○ UV mapping is the process of projecting a 2D image onto a 3D model.

○ Proper UV unwrapping prevents texture stretching and distortion.

○ Tools like Blender, Substance Painter, and UVLayout help refine UV maps.

4. **Rigging and Animation**

○ AR and VR often involve animated characters and objects.

○ Rigging involves creating a skeleton for a model to allow movement.

○ Keyframe animation and inverse kinematics (IK) enhance realism.

5. **Level of Detail (LOD)**

○ LOD reduces the complexity of models when viewed from a distance.

○ This technique improves rendering efficiency in AR and VR applications.

Tools for 3D Modeling in AR & VR

SEVERAL TOOLS EXIST for creating and optimizing 3D assets for AR and VR. Some of the most popular include:

- **Blender** – Open-source 3D modeling, sculpting, texturing, and animation tool.
- **Autodesk Maya** – Industry-standard software for high-end 3D modeling and animation.
- **3ds Max** – Commonly used in game development and architectural visualization.
- **ZBrush** – Best suited for digital sculpting and high-detail character modeling.
- **Substance Painter** – Used for texturing and material creation with PBR workflows.

Asset Optimization for AR & VR

OPTIMIZING 3D MODELS ensures smooth performance in AR and VR applications. Here are essential optimization techniques:

Polygon Reduction

REDUCING POLYGON COUNT without sacrificing detail improves performance. Techniques include:

- Using decimation tools in Blender or Maya.
- Retopology to create a low-poly version of a high-poly model.
- Using LOD techniques to display different levels of detail based on camera distance.

Texture Optimization

- Use compressed texture formats (e.g., JPG, WebP) for mobile AR and VR applications.
- Reduce texture resolution where possible (e.g., 1024x1024 instead of 4096x4096).
- Implement texture atlases to minimize draw calls.

Efficient UV Mapping

- Minimize seams to avoid visible texture distortions.
- Use non-overlapping UVs for PBR textures.
- Optimize UV packing to maximize texture usage.

Normal Maps and Baked Lighting

- Normal maps add surface detail without increasing polygon count.
- Baked lighting reduces real-time rendering calculations by precomputing light effects.

Implementing 3D Models in AR & VR Development

AFTER CREATING AND optimizing 3D models, they need to be imported into AR/VR development environments like Unity or Unreal Engine.

Importing 3D Models into Unity

UNITY SUPPORTS VARIOUS 3D file formats, including FBX, OBJ, and GLTF. To import a model:

1. Place the .fbx or .obj file into the Unity Assets folder.
2. Configure material settings under the **Inspector** panel.
3. Adjust lighting and shadows to enhance realism.

Example: Importing an FBX Model in Unity

```
USING UNITYENGINE;

public class Load3DModel : MonoBehaviour

{

public GameObject modelPrefab;

void Start()
```

```
{
Instantiate(modelPrefab, new Vector3(0, 0, 0), Quaternion.identity);
}
}
```

Importing 3D Models into Unreal Engine

UNREAL ENGINE USES the FBX format for 3D models. The import process:

1. Open the **Content Browser** in Unreal Engine.
2. Click **Import**, then select the .fbx file.
3. Configure material and LOD settings.

Best Practices for 3D Asset Creation in AR & VR

TO ENSURE OPTIMAL PERFORMANCE and quality, follow these best practices:

- **Keep polycounts optimized** – Aim for under 100K polygons for AR models, and under 1M for VR environments.

- **Use efficient materials** – Minimize the number of materials per model.

- **Bake lighting when possible** – Reduces real-time performance costs.

- **Test on target hardware** – Performance varies between mobile and PC-based AR/VR devices.

- **Follow platform-specific guidelines** – Each AR/VR platform has performance and compatibility requirements.

Conclusion

3D MODELING AND ASSET creation play a crucial role in AR and VR development. By optimizing polygon count, textures, and lighting, developers can create high-quality assets that run efficiently across different devices. Leveraging tools like Blender, Unity, and Unreal Engine ensures that assets integrate seamlessly into immersive AR and VR experiences. Understanding these principles enables developers to craft compelling and performant digital environments that enhance user engagement.

Interaction Design and User Interfaces in AR & VR

INTERACTION DESIGN is a critical aspect of Augmented Reality (AR) and Virtual Reality (VR) development, ensuring that users can effectively engage with digital content in an intuitive and immersive manner. Unlike traditional 2D applications, AR and VR interactions involve spatial environments, 3D interfaces, and different input modalities. This section explores the principles of interaction design, UI components, best practices, and tools for developing intuitive user experiences in AR and VR.

Principles of Interaction Design in AR & VR

INTERACTION DESIGN in AR and VR follows several key principles:

- **Spatial Awareness**: AR and VR applications take place in a 3D environment, requiring interfaces that respect real-world depth, perspective, and spatial positioning.

- **Intuitive Interactions**: Users should be able to interact naturally with objects through gestures, eye tracking, voice commands, or controllers.

- **Immersion**: The user interface (UI) should feel integrated into the environment rather than appearing as a separate overlay.

- **User Comfort**: Avoid excessive motion, unnatural movements, or abrupt transitions that can cause motion sickness or disorientation.

- **Feedback and Responsiveness**: Every user action should have clear feedback, such as haptic responses, visual cues, or auditory signals.

User Interface Components in AR & VR

AR AND VR USER INTERFACES differ significantly from traditional 2D applications. Below are key UI components used in immersive environments:

1. Menus and Panels

- Floating menus are commonly used in VR, positioned within the user's field of view.

- In AR, menus can be anchored to real-world objects or appear as hand-held interfaces.

- Panels should be placed at an optimal distance (1-2 meters in VR) for readability.

2. Buttons and Interaction Elements

- Physical-like buttons with depth and hover effects provide better affordance in VR.

- Hand-tracking allows direct interaction with buttons without controllers.

- Gaze-based selection enables hands-free interaction.

3. Tooltips and Visual Cues

- Holographic tooltips guide users without breaking immersion.

- Icons and floating indicators help users locate interactive objects.

- Reticles (crosshair-like indicators) assist with gaze-based selections.

4. Hand and Controller-Based Interaction

- VR systems like Oculus and SteamVR use controllers for pointing, grabbing, and selecting.

- AR hand-tracking enables natural gestures like pinching and swiping.

5. Voice Commands and AI Assistants

- Voice-controlled UI enables hands-free interaction, especially useful for enterprise and accessibility applications.

- AI-driven assistants can provide real-time guidance and contextual information.

Designing UI for AR & VR

WHEN DESIGNING INTERFACES for AR and VR, consider the following approaches:

1. Diegetic vs. Non-Diegetic UI

- **Diegetic UI**: Elements that exist naturally in the environment (e.g., holographic controls on a machine in AR, or a dashboard inside a VR cockpit).

- **Non-Diegetic UI**: Floating menus and HUDs that do not belong to the scene (commonly used for system settings).

- **Meta UI**: External interfaces such as controller status indicators.

- **Spatial UI**: Floating panels that adapt to user positioning and movement.

2. Depth and Layering

- UI elements should be positioned at appropriate depths to prevent eye strain.

- Avoid placing UI elements too close (less than 50 cm) or too far (beyond 3 meters).

- Use subtle shadows and occlusion to improve depth perception.

3. Interaction Methods

DIFFERENT INTERACTION models suit different use cases:

- **Direct Interaction**: Users touch or grab virtual objects directly.

- **Raycasting**: Users point at objects with a laser-like beam (common in VR).

- **Gaze-Based Selection**: Users select items by looking at them.

- **Gesture-Based Interaction**: Users perform gestures like swiping, pinching, or grabbing.

Implementing AR & VR UI in Unity

UNITY PROVIDES POWERFUL tools for designing and implementing AR/VR interfaces. Below is an example of implementing a floating UI panel in VR using Unity's XR Toolkit.

Creating a Floating UI Panel in VR

1. Import the **XR Interaction Toolkit** package in Unity.
2. Create a **Canvas** and set its **Render Mode** to **World Space**.
3. Attach an **XR Interactable UI Component** to enable interactions.

Example: Creating a Floating UI Panel in Unity

```
USING UNITYENGINE;
using UnityEngine.UI;
public class FloatingPanel : MonoBehaviour
{
public Transform cameraTransform;
public float followSpeed = 2.0f;
void Update()
{
// Make the panel face the user
transform.LookAt(cameraTransform.position);
transform.Rotate(0, 180, 0);
}
}
```

- This script ensures that the UI panel always faces the user, improving accessibility.

Implementing Gaze-Based Interaction

GAZE-BASED INTERACTION allows users to select UI elements by looking at them.

Example: Implementing Gaze Interaction

```
USING UNITYENGINE;
public class GazeInteract : MonoBehaviour
{
private float gazeTime = 0;
public float gazeThreshold = 2.0f;
void Update()
{
if (IsUserLookingAtObject())
{
gazeTime += Time.deltaTime;
if (gazeTime >= gazeThreshold)
{
TriggerInteraction();
}
}
else
{
gazeTime = 0;
}
```

```
}
private bool IsUserLookingAtObject()
{
// Implement raycasting logic here
return true; // Placeholder
}
private void TriggerInteraction()
{
Debug.Log("Object selected via gaze interaction!");
}
}
```

- This script detects if the user is gazing at an object for a set duration and triggers an interaction.

Best Practices for AR & VR UI Design

TO CREATE USER-FRIENDLY interfaces in AR and VR, follow these best practices:

1. **Minimize Clutter**: Too many UI elements can overwhelm users and reduce immersion.
2. **Avoid Fixed HUDs**: Instead of static heads-up displays, use context-sensitive overlays.
3. **Use Animation and Transitions**: Smooth animations improve usability and user engagement.
4. **Provide Clear Feedback**: Use sound, haptics, and visual

effects to confirm user actions.

5. **Optimize for Performance**: Avoid complex UI elements that slow down rendering.
6. **Ensure Accessibility**: Support alternative interaction methods like voice control.

Future Trends in AR & VR UI Design

AS AR AND VR EVOLVE, new UI paradigms are emerging:

- **AI-Powered Interfaces**: Intelligent assistants that adapt to user behavior.

- **Brain-Computer Interfaces (BCI)**: Neural input for controlling interfaces.

- **Haptic Feedback**: Advanced touch-based interactions using wearables.

- **Spatial AI**: Environments that react dynamically to user presence.

Conclusion

DESIGNING EFFECTIVE UI and interactions in AR and VR requires an understanding of spatial environments, intuitive controls, and immersive elements. By leveraging 3D UI components, gaze-based interactions, voice commands, and optimized performance techniques, developers can create seamless and engaging experiences. Future advancements in AI, haptics, and spatial computing will continue to shape how users interact with AR and VR interfaces.

Motion Tracking and Sensor Integration

MOTION TRACKING AND sensor integration are fundamental to creating immersive Augmented Reality (AR) and Virtual Reality (VR) experiences. These technologies enable devices to track a user's position, orientation, and interactions within a virtual space, ensuring realistic and responsive experiences. In this section, we will explore the different types of motion tracking, sensors used in AR/VR, key integration techniques, and best practices for developing applications with accurate motion tracking.

Types of Motion Tracking

MOTION TRACKING CAN be broadly categorized into **positional tracking** and **rotational tracking**, both of which are critical for AR and VR experiences.

1. Positional Tracking (6DOF)

POSITIONAL TRACKING determines the physical location of the user or device in a 3D environment. It includes:

- **Inside-out tracking**: Uses built-in cameras and sensors to track the environment (e.g., Oculus Quest, ARKit, ARCore).
- **Outside-in tracking**: Uses external sensors or cameras to track the headset or controllers (e.g., HTC Vive Lighthouse tracking).

2. Rotational Tracking (3DOF)

ROTATIONAL TRACKING measures the orientation (pitch, yaw, and roll) of a device or controller but does not track actual movement in space.

- Commonly used in mobile-based VR headsets (e.g., Google Cardboard).
- Uses gyroscopes and accelerometers for head rotation tracking.

3. Marker-Based Tracking

MARKER-BASED TRACKING uses predefined visual markers (such as QR codes or AR markers) to determine the position and orientation of the camera.

- Used in AR applications to anchor virtual objects to real-world locations.
- Works with SDKs like **Vuforia, ARKit**, and **ARCore**.

4. Markerless Tracking (SLAM - Simultaneous Localization and Mapping)

- Uses computer vision algorithms to map the environment dynamically.
- Enables AR applications to track surfaces and objects without predefined markers.
- Examples: Apple's ARKit, Google's ARCore, and Microsoft's HoloLens.

Sensors Used in AR & VR

MOTION TRACKING RELIES on a combination of sensors to provide accurate positioning and orientation data. These sensors include:

1. Inertial Measurement Unit (IMU)

AN IMU CONSISTS OF:

- **Accelerometer**: Measures linear acceleration in x, y, and z directions.
- **Gyroscope**: Measures angular velocity for rotational tracking.
- **Magnetometer**: Detects orientation relative to the Earth's magnetic field.

IMUs are widely used in VR controllers, AR headsets, and smartphones to track motion.

2. Depth Sensors (LiDAR, Time-of-Flight Sensors)

DEPTH SENSORS MEASURE the distance between objects and the device, enabling accurate depth perception for AR experiences.

- **LiDAR (Light Detection and Ranging)**: Used in iPhones, iPads, and AR headsets for object and environment scanning.
- **Time-of-Flight (ToF) Cameras**: Measure the time light takes to return, improving real-time AR tracking.

3. Optical Tracking Cameras

- Track movements using infrared or RGB cameras.
- Used in VR tracking systems like Oculus Insight and HTC Vive's Lighthouse.

4. Hand Tracking Sensors

- Enable interaction without controllers (e.g., Leap Motion, Meta Quest hand tracking).
- Use machine learning to detect and track hand gestures.

Implementing Motion Tracking in AR/VR Applications

TO INTEGRATE MOTION tracking into AR and VR applications, developers use SDKs and frameworks such as Unity's XR Toolkit, ARKit, and ARCore.

1. Head Tracking in Unity VR Applications

UNITY PROVIDES BUILT-in support for head tracking through XR plugins.

Example: Retrieving Headset Position and Rotation in Unity

```
USING UNITYENGINE;

using UnityEngine.XR;

public class HeadTracking : MonoBehaviour
```

```
{
void Update()
{
Vector3 headPosition =
InputTracking.GetLocalPosition(XRNode.Head);
Quaternion headRotation =
InputTracking.GetLocalRotation(XRNode.Head);
transform.position = headPosition;
transform.rotation = headRotation;
}
}
```

- This script continuously updates the position and rotation of an object based on the user's head movement in a VR environment.

2. Implementing Hand Tracking in Unity

HAND TRACKING ALLOWS users to interact with virtual objects naturally.

Example: Detecting Hand Presence in Unity XR Toolkit

```
USING UNITYENGINE;
using UnityEngine.XR.Interaction.Toolkit;
public class HandTracking : MonoBehaviour
```

```
{
public XRController leftHand;
public XRController rightHand;
void Update()
{
if (leftHand.inputDevice.isValid)
{
Debug.Log("Left hand detected");
}
if (rightHand.inputDevice.isValid)
{
Debug.Log("Right hand detected");
}
}
}
```

- This script detects whether the user's left or right hand is being tracked by the VR system.

3. Object Tracking in AR using ARKit (iOS)

ARKIT ENABLES MARKERLESS tracking using real-world objects and surfaces.

Example: Placing an AR Object on a Surface using ARKit

```
IMPORT ARKIT

import SceneKit

class ARObjectPlacer: UIViewController, ARSCNViewDelegate {

@IBOutlet var sceneView: ARSCNView!

override func viewDidLoad() {

super.viewDidLoad()

sceneView.delegate = self

sceneView.session.run(ARWorldTrackingConfiguration())

}

func placeObject(at location: ARRaycastResult) {

let sphere = SCNSphere(radius: 0.05)

let node = SCNNode(geometry: sphere)

node.position                                              =
SCNVector3(location.worldTransform.columns.3.x,

location.worldTransform.columns.3.y,

location.worldTransform.columns.3.z)

sceneView.scene.rootNode.addChildNode(node)

}

}
```

- This Swift code detects surfaces and places a 3D object in AR using Apple's ARKit.

Challenges in Motion Tracking

DESPITE ADVANCEMENTS in motion tracking, developers face several challenges:

1. **Drift and Latency**:

   ○ IMU sensors can drift over time, causing inaccurate tracking.

   ○ Latency in data processing affects responsiveness.

2. **Occlusion and Environmental Limitations**:

   ○ Optical tracking may fail when objects or hands are obstructed.

   ○ Poor lighting conditions can reduce tracking accuracy.

3. **Battery Consumption**:

   ○ Continuous sensor processing consumes power, affecting mobile AR/VR applications.

4. **Calibration Issues**:

   ○ Improper calibration can lead to tracking inaccuracies.

   ○ Frequent recalibration may be required for precise motion tracking.

Best Practices for Motion Tracking and Sensor Integration

TO ACHIEVE ACCURATE motion tracking in AR and VR applications, developers should follow these best practices:

- **Optimize Sensor Fusion**: Combine data from multiple sensors (IMU, depth sensors, cameras) for improved accuracy.
- **Reduce Latency**: Use high-performance frameworks and low-latency networking for real-time tracking.
- **Implement Predictive Algorithms**: Use AI and Kalman filters to predict user movements and compensate for tracking errors.
- **Ensure Robust Environment Mapping**: Use SLAM techniques to adapt to different environments dynamically.
- **Minimize Motion Sickness**: Avoid sudden movements, unnatural accelerations, and large positional jumps in VR applications.

Future Trends in Motion Tracking

THE FUTURE OF AR AND VR motion tracking is evolving with advancements in AI, 5G, and wearable technologies. Key trends include:

- **AI-Powered Pose Estimation**: Machine learning models that improve body tracking without additional hardware.

- **Neural Interfaces**: Brain-computer interfaces (BCI) for direct neural interaction.

- **Wearable Sensors**: Smart gloves and haptic suits for full-body motion tracking.

- **Cloud-Based Tracking**: Offloading tracking computations to cloud servers for better efficiency.

Conclusion

MOTION TRACKING AND sensor integration are essential components of AR and VR applications, enabling realistic and immersive interactions. By leveraging IMUs, depth sensors, and optical tracking, developers can create more natural and responsive experiences. As technology advances, motion tracking will continue to improve, pushing the boundaries of AR and VR innovation.

Optimizing Performance and Latency in AR & VR

OPTIMIZING PERFORMANCE and minimizing latency are crucial for delivering smooth and immersive experiences in Augmented Reality (AR) and Virtual Reality (VR) applications. High latency and performance issues can cause motion sickness, lag, and reduced interactivity, significantly impacting user experience. This section explores techniques for improving rendering efficiency, reducing latency, optimizing assets, and ensuring real-time performance in AR and VR applications.

Understanding Performance Bottlenecks in AR & VR

PERFORMANCE ISSUES in AR and VR arise due to various factors, including hardware limitations, inefficient rendering, unoptimized assets, and network latency. Some common bottlenecks include:

- **High polygon count and unoptimized 3D models**
- **Inefficient texture and shader usage**
- **Excessive draw calls and complex scene rendering**
- **Slow tracking and sensor processing**
- **Network latency in multiplayer or cloud-based applications**

To maintain a seamless experience, AR and VR applications should aim for:

- **90+ FPS for VR headsets** to prevent motion sickness.
- **60 FPS for mobile AR applications** to ensure smooth tracking.
- **Low motion-to-photon latency (below 20ms)** for real-time interactions.

Rendering Optimization Techniques

EFFICIENT RENDERING is essential for maintaining high frame rates in AR and VR applications. Key techniques include:

1. Level of Detail (LOD) Management

USING LOD TECHNIQUES can significantly improve performance by reducing the complexity of distant objects.

- Implement multiple LODs for 3D models, where:
  - LOD0: High-detail model for close proximity.
  - LOD1: Medium-detail model for mid-range.
  - LOD2: Low-detail model for distant rendering.

Example: Unity LOD Implementation

```
USING UNITYENGINE;

public class LODSwitcher : MonoBehaviour

{

public LODGroup lodGroup;

void Start()

{

lodGroup = GetComponent<LODGroup>();

}

}
```

- Unity's **LODGroup** component automatically switches between different levels of detail based on the camera's distance.

2. Occlusion Culling

RENDERING OBJECTS THAT are not visible to the user wastes resources. Occlusion culling prevents this by ensuring only visible objects are processed.

Unity Example: Enabling Occlusion Culling

```
CAMERA.MAIN.USEOCCLUSIONCULLING = true;
```

- This setting reduces the rendering workload by not drawing objects blocked by other geometry.

3. Frustum Culling

FRUSTUM CULLING ENSURES that only objects within the camera's view are rendered, preventing unnecessary draw calls.

Example: Implementing Frustum Culling in Unity

```
USING UNITYENGINE;

public class FrustumCulling : MonoBehaviour

{

void Update()

{

Plane[] frustumPlanes = GeometryUtility.CalculateFrustumPlanes(Camera.main);

Collider[] objects = FindObjectsOfType<Collider>();
```

```
foreach (Collider obj in objects)
{
if (GeometryUtility.TestPlanesAABB(frustumPlanes, obj.bounds))
{
obj.gameObject.SetActive(true);
}
else
{
obj.gameObject.SetActive(false);
}
}
}
}
```

- This script disables objects that fall outside the camera's frustum, improving performance.

Asset Optimization

ASSET OPTIMIZATION reduces the computational load on AR and VR applications.

1. Reducing Polygon Count in 3D Models

- Use **low-poly models** and rely on **normal maps** for detail.

• Convert high-poly assets into optimized versions using Blender or Unity's **ProBuilder**.

2. Texture Compression and Atlas Mapping

• Use compressed texture formats such as **ASTC, ETC2, or BC7**.

• Implement **texture atlases** to group multiple textures into a single file, reducing memory usage.

Example: Using Texture Atlases in Unity

```
MATERIAL ATLASMATERIAL = Resources.Load<Material>("AtlasMaterial");

gameObject.GetComponent<Renderer>().material = atlasMaterial;
```

• This script applies a preloaded texture atlas to an object's material, reducing texture swaps.

3. Shader Optimization

• Use **unlit shaders** for objects that do not require complex lighting.

• Optimize **PBR materials** by reducing unnecessary reflections and complex effects.

Example: Unity Unlit Shader

```
SHADER "CUSTOM/UNLITSHADER"
```

```
{
SubShader
{
Tags { "RenderType"="Opaque" }
Pass
{
Lighting Off
}
}
}
```

- Unlit shaders improve performance by skipping lighting calculations.

Minimizing Latency

REDUCING LATENCY IS critical for responsive interactions in AR and VR.

1. Asynchronous Timewarp (ATW) and Spacewarp

- ATW reduces perceived latency by adjusting the last rendered frame based on head movement.
- Spacewarp generates intermediate frames to maintain smooth motion.
- Available in Oculus SDK and SteamVR.

2. Predictive Tracking

- Uses AI and sensor fusion to estimate future movements.
- Reduces input lag for controllers and headsets.

Example: Implementing Predictive Tracking in Unity

VECTOR3 PREDICTEDPOSITION = currentPosition + (velocity * Time.deltaTime);

transform.position = predictedPosition;

- This estimates future positions based on current velocity to reduce perceived lag.

3. Reducing Motion-to-Photon Latency

- Optimize the rendering pipeline by minimizing CPU-GPU bottlenecks.
- Enable **fixed foveated rendering (FFR)** to reduce GPU load in peripheral vision.

Network Optimization for AR/VR

FOR CLOUD-BASED OR multiplayer AR/VR applications, optimizing network performance is essential.

1. Edge Computing for AR/VR

- Offload rendering and tracking calculations to **edge servers.**

- Reduces latency compared to cloud-based processing.

2. WebRTC for Low-Latency Streaming

- Use **WebRTC** for real-time AR/VR streaming with minimal delay.

Example: Implementing WebRTC in Unity

```
USING UNITY.WEBRTC;
```

- WebRTC enables low-latency communication in AR/VR multiplayer experiences.

3. Adaptive Bitrate Streaming

- Dynamically adjust video quality based on bandwidth to prevent lag.

Best Practices for AR & VR Performance Optimization

- **Optimize draw calls**: Reduce the number of objects rendered per frame.
- **Use GPU instancing**: Batch-render similar objects to reduce CPU overhead.
- **Avoid overdraw**: Minimize transparent and overlapping objects to reduce rendering load.
- **Utilize fixed frame timing**: Ensure consistent rendering to prevent jitter.

- **Profile and debug regularly**: Use tools like **Unity Profiler, Oculus Debug Tool, and RenderDoc** to identify bottlenecks.

Future Trends in AR & VR Optimization

- **AI-driven rendering optimizations**: Machine learning models to predict and pre-render frames.
- **5G and low-latency cloud rendering**: Offloading graphics processing to edge computing servers.
- **Neural rendering**: Using AI-generated imagery for hyper-realistic experiences.

Conclusion

OPTIMIZING PERFORMANCE and latency in AR and VR applications is essential to delivering smooth, immersive, and responsive experiences. By leveraging rendering techniques, reducing asset complexity, minimizing latency, and optimizing network performance, developers can enhance the efficiency and quality of their AR/VR applications. As technology advances, new optimization strategies will continue to push the boundaries of real-time interactive experiences.

Chapter 4: Developing Augmented Reality Applications

AR SDKs: ARKit, ARCore, and Vuforia

AUGMENTED REALITY (AR) development relies on robust Software Development Kits (SDKs) that provide the necessary tools and frameworks for creating immersive and interactive AR applications. The three most widely used AR SDKs are **ARKit (Apple)**, **ARCore (Google)**, and **Vuforia (PTC)**. Each of these SDKs offers unique features, capabilities, and support for different platforms. This section explores their features, differences, and use cases in AR development.

Understanding AR SDKs

AR SDKS ENABLE DEVELOPERS to integrate augmented reality features into applications by leveraging device hardware such as cameras, accelerometers, gyroscopes, and LiDAR sensors. These SDKs handle **computer vision, motion tracking, plane detection, object recognition, and spatial mapping**, allowing developers to focus on building engaging user experiences.

ARKit (Apple)

ARKIT IS APPLE'S AR development framework designed exclusively for iOS devices. It provides a high-level API that integrates AR capabilities into iOS applications using Swift or Objective-C.

Key Features of ARKit

- **World Tracking**: Uses Visual Inertial Odometry (VIO) to track device movement in 3D space.
- **Plane Detection**: Identifies horizontal and vertical surfaces for placing virtual objects.
- **LiDAR Support**: Utilizes LiDAR sensors on newer iPhones and iPads for enhanced depth perception and occlusion.
- **Face Tracking**: Supports advanced facial recognition and AR-based face filters.
- **Object Recognition**: Recognizes 3D objects and images for interactive experiences.
- **People Occlusion**: Allows virtual objects to realistically interact with real-world people.

Example: ARKit SceneKit Integration

```
IMPORT ARKIT

import SceneKit

import UIKit

class ViewController: UIViewController, ARSCNViewDelegate {

@IBOutlet var sceneView: ARSCNView!

override func viewDidLoad() {

super.viewDidLoad()
```

```
sceneView.delegate = self
sceneView.session.run(ARWorldTrackingConfiguration())
addVirtualObject()
}
func addVirtualObject() {
let sphere = SCNSphere(radius: 0.1)
let material = SCNMaterial()
material.diffuse.contents = UIColor.blue
sphere.materials = [material]
let node = SCNNode()
node.position = SCNVector3(0, 0, -0.5)
node.geometry = sphere
sceneView.scene.rootNode.addChildNode(node)
}
}
```

This example demonstrates how to use **ARKit with SceneKit** to place a simple blue sphere in an AR scene.

ARCore (Google)

ARCORE IS GOOGLE'S AR development platform designed for **Android and Web-based AR experiences**. It provides similar functionality to ARKit but is optimized for a broader range of Android devices.

Key Features of ARCore

- **Motion Tracking**: Uses camera input and sensor data to track the device's position.
- **Environmental Understanding**: Detects and maps horizontal and vertical surfaces.
- **Light Estimation**: Adjusts virtual object lighting based on real-world conditions.
- **Augmented Images**: Recognizes 2D images and augments them with virtual content.
- **Cloud Anchors**: Enables persistent and shared AR experiences across multiple devices.

Example: ARCore Sceneform Integration

```
PUBLIC CLASS MAINACTIVITY extends AppCompatActivity
{

private ArFragment arFragment;

@Override

protected void onCreate(Bundle savedInstanceState) {

super.onCreate(savedInstanceState);

setContentView(R.layout.activity_main);

arFragment = (ArFragment)
getSupportFragmentManager().findFragmentById(R.id.ar_fragment);
```

```
arFragment.setOnTapArPlaneListener((hitResult, plane, motionEvent) -> {

Anchor anchor = hitResult.createAnchor();

placeObject(arFragment, anchor, Uri.parse("model.sfb"));

});

}

private void placeObject(ArFragment arFragment, Anchor anchor, Uri modelUri) {

ModelRenderable.builder()

.setSource(this, modelUri)

.build()

.thenAccept(modelRenderable -> addNodeToScene(arFragment, anchor, modelRenderable))

.exceptionally(throwable -> {

Log.e("ARCore", "Error loading 3D model", throwable);

return null;

});

}

private void addNodeToScene(ArFragment fragment, Anchor anchor, ModelRenderable modelRenderable) {

AnchorNode anchorNode = new AnchorNode(anchor);
```

```
TransformableNode node = new TransformableNode(fragment.getTransformationSystem());

node.setRenderable(modelRenderable);

node.setParent(anchorNode);

fragment.getArSceneView().getScene().addChild(anchorNode);

node.select();

}

}
```

This code shows how to use **ARCore with Sceneform** to place a 3D model in an AR environment when the user taps on a detected surface.

Vuforia (PTC)

VUFORIA IS A POWERFUL AR SDK focused on **image recognition, object tracking, and model targets**. It supports both **iOS and Android** and is widely used in industrial applications, training, and marketing.

Key Features of Vuforia

- **Image Targets**: Recognizes and augments predefined images.
- **Object Recognition**: Identifies and tracks 3D objects.
- **VuMarks**: Custom visual markers that function as QR codes for AR.

- **Cloud Recognition**: Uses cloud-based databases for scalable object recognition.
- **Model Targets**: Recognizes and tracks CAD-based 3D models.

Example: Vuforia in Unity (C#)

```
USING UNITYENGINE;

using Vuforia;

public class ARInteraction : MonoBehaviour, ITrackableEventHandler {

private TrackableBehaviour trackableBehaviour;

void Start() {

trackableBehaviour = GetComponent<TrackableBehaviour>();

if (trackableBehaviour) {

trackableBehaviour.RegisterTrackableEventHandler(this);

}

}

public void OnTrackableStateChanged(TrackableBehaviour.Status previousStatus, TrackableBehaviour.Status newStatus) {

if (newStatus == TrackableBehaviour.Status.TRACKED) {

Debug.Log("Object recognized!");

gameObject.SetActive(true);
```

```
} else {
gameObject.SetActive(false);
}
}
}
```

This script uses **Vuforia's tracking system** to activate a virtual object when a tracked image or model is recognized.

Choosing the Right AR SDK

Feature	ARKit (iOS)	ARCore (Android)	Vuforia (Cross-platform)
Platform	iOS	Android	iOS, Android, Unity, HoloLens
Tracking	VIO + LiDAR	VIO + Camera	Image, Object, Cloud
Plane Detection	Yes	Yes	Limited
Face Tracking	Yes	Limited	No
Cloud Anchors	No	Yes	Yes
Best For	iOS apps, AR games	Android apps, persistent AR	Image tracking, industrial AR

Conclusion

CHOOSING AN AR SDK depends on the project's platform, features, and requirements.

- **Use ARKit** if developing for **iOS** with a focus on high-performance AR.
- **Use ARCore** for **Android** applications with broader device support.
- **Use Vuforia** for **image-based tracking** or **cross-platform solutions.**

Each of these SDKs provides extensive tools and libraries, making it possible to create **interactive, immersive, and high-performance AR applications** tailored to different industries and use cases.

Marker-Based vs. Markerless AR

AUGMENTED REALITY (AR) applications rely on different tracking techniques to overlay digital content onto the real world. The two primary methods used for AR tracking are **marker-based AR** and **markerless AR.** Each approach has its own strengths and is suited for different types of AR experiences.

This section explores **marker-based AR, markerless AR,** their use cases, and how to implement them in AR development using popular AR SDKs.

Marker-Based AR

MARKER-BASED AR, ALSO known as **image recognition AR,** relies on predefined **visual markers** (such as QR codes, printed images, or symbols) to anchor virtual objects in the real world. The AR application detects these markers using the camera and superimposes digital content onto them.

How Marker-Based AR Works

1. The camera scans the environment to detect a **predefined marker**.
2. The AR SDK processes the marker's **unique pattern** and calculates its position and orientation.
3. A **virtual object** is rendered on top of the marker, maintaining its position as long as the marker is in view.

Advantages of Marker-Based AR

- **High Precision**: Since the marker is predefined, AR objects are anchored accurately.

- **Low Processing Power**: Less computationally demanding compared to markerless AR.

- **Better Stability**: Objects remain fixed in place relative to the marker.

Disadvantages of Marker-Based AR

- **Requires Physical Markers**: Users must have printed images or QR codes.

- **Limited Interaction**: The AR experience is tied to specific markers.

- **Not Suitable for Large-Scale AR**: Cannot be used for world-scale tracking.

Example: Implementing Marker-Based AR with Vuforia in Unity

```
USING UNITYENGINE;

using Vuforia;

public class MarkerAR : MonoBehaviour, ITrackableEventHandler {

private TrackableBehaviour trackableBehaviour;

void Start() {

trackableBehaviour = GetComponent<TrackableBehaviour>();

if (trackableBehaviour) {

trackableBehaviour.RegisterTrackableEventHandler(this);

}

}

public void OnTrackableStateChanged(TrackableBehaviour.Status previousStatus, TrackableBehaviour.Status newStatus) {

if (newStatus == TrackableBehaviour.Status.TRACKED) {

Debug.Log("Marker detected!");

gameObject.SetActive(true);

} else {

gameObject.SetActive(false);

}

}
```

```
}
```

This script uses **Vuforia** to detect a marker and display a virtual object when the marker is found.

Markerless AR

MARKERLESS AR, ALSO known as **location-based or world-tracking AR**, does not require predefined markers. Instead, it relies on **device sensors, GPS, accelerometers, and SLAM (Simultaneous Localization and Mapping)** to place virtual objects in the environment.

How Markerless AR Works

1. The AR system **analyzes the environment** using the camera feed and motion sensors.
2. It detects **surfaces, depth, and real-world features** to establish an anchor point.
3. Virtual objects are **placed and persist** even if the user moves the camera.

Advantages of Markerless AR

- **More Flexibility**: Users can place AR objects anywhere without printed markers.

- **Better User Experience**: Allows **interactive AR applications** such as navigation and gaming.

- **Supports Large-Scale AR**: Suitable for outdoor AR experiences and **persistent AR**.

Disadvantages of Markerless AR

- **Higher Processing Power**: Requires **real-time depth and motion tracking**, consuming more battery.
- **Less Accuracy**: Virtual objects may drift due to **sensor limitations.**
- **Requires More Development Effort**: SLAM-based tracking is complex compared to marker-based AR.

Example: Implementing Markerless AR with ARKit in Swift

```
IMPORT ARKIT

import SceneKit

import UIKit

class ViewController: UIViewController, ARSCNViewDelegate {

@IBOutlet var sceneView: ARSCNView!

override func viewDidLoad() {

super.viewDidLoad()

sceneView.delegate = self

sceneView.session.run(ARWorldTrackingConfiguration())

addVirtualObject()

}

func addVirtualObject() {
```

```
let cube = SCNBox(width: 0.1, height: 0.1, length: 0.1, chamferRadius: 0)

let material = SCNMaterial()

material.diffuse.contents = UIColor.red

cube.materials = [material]

let node = SCNNode()

node.position = SCNVector3(0, 0, -0.5)

node.geometry = cube

sceneView.scene.rootNode.addChildNode(node)

}

}
```

This **ARKit example** demonstrates how to create a **markerless AR experience** by placing a **virtual cube** in the environment.

Comparison of Marker-Based vs. Markerless AR

Feature	Marker-Based AR	Markerless AR
Tracking	Uses predefined markers	Uses SLAM and sensors
Setup	Requires physical markers	No markers needed
Accuracy	High (marker is a fixed reference)	Lower (depends on real-world tracking)
Processing Power	Low	High
Best For	Product packaging, AR books, museums	Games, navigation, large-scale AR

Use Cases of Marker-Based and Markerless AR

Marker-Based AR Applications

- **Retail & Marketing**: Companies use **printed AR markers** to display **interactive product ads.**
- **Education**: Textbooks with **AR markers** allow students to visualize concepts.
- **Industrial Training**: Workers scan markers to receive **step-by-step AR instructions.**

Markerless AR Applications

- **AR Navigation**: Apps like **Google AR Navigation** overlay directional arrows in real-world environments.
- **AR Gaming**: Games such as **Pokémon GO** use markerless tracking for placing virtual creatures.
- **Interior Design**: Apps like **IKEA Place** allow users to preview furniture in their homes.

Implementing Marker-Based and Markerless AR in Unity

UNITY SUPPORTS **both marker-based and markerless AR** via the **AR Foundation** framework, which integrates with **ARKit and ARCore**.

Marker-Based AR in Unity

TO IMPLEMENT **marker-based AR** in Unity:

1. **Install Vuforia SDK** and import it into Unity.
2. **Create an Image Target** and assign a reference image.
3. **Attach virtual content** that appears when the marker is detected.

Markerless AR in Unity

TO IMPLEMENT **markerless AR** in Unity using AR Foundation:

1. **Enable ARCore/ARKit** support in Unity's XR settings.
2. **Use ARRaycastManager** to detect surfaces.
3. **Place virtual objects dynamically** at touch points.

Example: Markerless AR in Unity using AR Foundation (C#)

```
USING UNITYENGINE;

using UnityEngine.XR.ARFoundation;

using UnityEngine.XR.ARSubsystems;

public class ARPlacement : MonoBehaviour {

public ARRaycastManager raycastManager;

public GameObject objectToPlace;

private List<ARRaycastHit> hits = new List<ARRaycastHit>();

void Update() {

if (Input.touchCount > 0) {

Touch touch = Input.GetTouch(0);
```

```
if (raycastManager.Raycast(touch.position, hits, TrackableType.PlaneWithinPolygon)) {

Pose hitPose = hits[0].pose;

Instantiate(objectToPlace, hitPose.position, hitPose.rotation);

}

}

}

}
```

This script enables **touch-based object placement** in an AR scene without markers.

Conclusion

- **Marker-Based AR** is ideal for applications that need **high accuracy and predefined anchors**.
- **Markerless AR** offers **greater freedom and interaction**, making it better for **games, navigation, and large-scale AR**.
- **AR SDKs like ARKit, ARCore, Vuforia, and AR Foundation** provide developers with powerful tools to create **both types of AR experiences**.

UNDERSTANDING THE DIFFERENCES between **marker-based and markerless AR** is crucial for choosing the right approach when building **immersive AR applications**.

Object Recognition and Spatial Mapping

OBJECT RECOGNITION and spatial mapping are essential techniques in augmented reality (AR) development. They enable AR applications to **identify real-world objects, map environments,** and **place digital content** in contextually meaningful ways. These features allow for **realistic AR interactions**, making AR applications more immersive and functional.

This section explores **object recognition** and **spatial mapping**, their importance in AR applications, and how to implement them using popular AR SDKs such as **ARKit, ARCore, and Vuforia**.

Object Recognition in AR

OBJECT RECOGNITION in AR refers to the ability of an application to **identify and track specific objects** in the real world. This is achieved through **computer vision** techniques, which analyze an object's **shape, texture, and color** to match it against a predefined database.

How Object Recognition Works

1. The **AR camera scans the environment** to capture real-world objects.
2. The AR SDK **analyzes the object's features**, comparing them to a stored database.
3. Once a match is found, the application **overlays digital content** onto the recognized object.

Applications of Object Recognition in AR

- **Retail & E-Commerce**: Virtual product visualization, where AR apps recognize an item and provide details.
- **Education & Museums**: Interactive learning by recognizing historical artifacts and displaying information.
- **Industrial Training**: AR overlays instructions when recognizing machinery or tools.

Implementing Object Recognition with Vuforia

VUFORIA PROVIDES ONE of the most **robust object recognition systems** for AR applications.

Steps to Implement Object Recognition in Unity with Vuforia

1. **Create an Object Database** in the Vuforia Developer Portal.
2. **Upload a 3D model** or scan the object to generate a recognition dataset.
3. **Import the database** into Unity and assign it to the AR scene.

Example: Vuforia Object Recognition in Unity (C#)

```
USING UNITYENGINE;

using Vuforia;
```

```
public class ObjectRecognitionHandler : MonoBehaviour,
ITrackableEventHandler {

private TrackableBehaviour trackableBehaviour;

void Start() {

trackableBehaviour = GetComponent<TrackableBehaviour>();

if (trackableBehaviour) {

trackableBehaviour.RegisterTrackableEventHandler(this);

}

}

public void OnTrackableStateChanged(TrackableBehaviour.Status
previousStatus, TrackableBehaviour.Status newStatus) {

if (newStatus == TrackableBehaviour.Status.TRACKED) {

Debug.Log("Object recognized!");

gameObject.SetActive(true);

} else {

gameObject.SetActive(false);

}

}

}
```

This script enables Vuforia to **detect a real-world object** and display an **AR overlay** when it is recognized.

Spatial Mapping in AR

SPATIAL MAPPING IS the process of **scanning and constructing a 3D representation of an environment** in real time. This allows AR applications to understand **physical surfaces, obstacles, and room geometry**, making AR experiences more interactive.

How Spatial Mapping Works

1. The AR camera **captures depth and environmental data** using LiDAR, stereo vision, or other sensors.
2. The AR SDK **analyzes surfaces, edges, and obstacles** to generate a **3D mesh** of the environment.
3. Virtual objects are **placed in contextually relevant locations** based on the mapped surfaces.

Applications of Spatial Mapping in AR

- **Indoor Navigation**: AR can map and guide users inside buildings.

- **Gaming & Entertainment**: Games that use real-world environments as interactive elements.

- **Architecture & Design**: AR allows users to visualize furniture or remodels within mapped spaces.

Implementing Spatial Mapping in ARKit

ARKIT PROVIDES **plane detection and spatial mapping** capabilities using **LiDAR and computer vision.**

Example: ARKit Plane Detection in Swift

```
IMPORT ARKIT

import SceneKit

import UIKit

class ViewController: UIViewController, ARSCNViewDelegate {

@IBOutlet var sceneView: ARSCNView!

override func viewDidLoad() {

super.viewDidLoad()

sceneView.delegate = self

sceneView.session.run(ARWorldTrackingConfiguration())

}

func renderer(_ renderer: SCNSceneRenderer, didAdd node: SCNNode, for anchor: ARAnchor) {

guard let planeAnchor = anchor as? ARPlaneAnchor else { return }

let plane = SCNPlane(width: CGFloat(planeAnchor.extent.x), height: CGFloat(planeAnchor.extent.z))

plane.materials.first?.diffuse.contents = UIColor.blue.withAlphaComponent(0.5)

let planeNode = SCNNode(geometry: plane)

planeNode.position = SCNVector3(planeAnchor.center.x, 0, planeAnchor.center.z)
```

```
planeNode.eulerAngles.x = -.pi / 2

node.addChildNode(planeNode)

}

}
```

This **ARKit example** detects **flat surfaces (tables, floors, walls)** and **overlays a blue grid**, indicating detected planes.

Combining Object Recognition and Spatial Mapping

MANY AR APPLICATIONS **combine both object recognition and spatial mapping** for enhanced experiences. For example:

- **AR Museums**: Recognize a **statue** and display AR content, while spatial mapping ensures accurate object placement.
- **Smart AR Assistants**: Identify **furniture** while mapping room dimensions to suggest design layouts.
- **AR Gaming**: Detect a **real-world toy** and place game elements around it based on spatial mapping.

Example: Markerless Object Placement with ARCore

USING **ARCore's environmental understanding**, we can **place objects dynamically** based on detected surfaces.

```
using UnityEngine;

using UnityEngine.XR.ARFoundation;

using UnityEngine.XR.ARSubsystems;
```

```
public class ARObjectPlacer : MonoBehaviour {
public ARRaycastManager raycastManager;
public GameObject objectPrefab;
private List<ARRaycastHit> hits = new List<ARRaycastHit>();
void Update() {
if (Input.touchCount > 0) {
Touch touch = Input.GetTouch(0);
if (raycastManager.Raycast(touch.position, hits, TrackableType.PlaneWithinPolygon)) {
Pose hitPose = hits[0].pose;
Instantiate(objectPrefab, hitPose.position, hitPose.rotation);
}
}
}
}
```

This Unity script allows users to **tap on detected surfaces** and **place virtual objects** dynamically using ARCore.

Comparison of Object Recognition and Spatial Mapping

Feature	Object Recognition	Spatial Mapping
Tracking Method	Predefined 3D models or images	Real-time environment scanning
Best For	Recognizing and tracking objects	Mapping rooms, detecting surfaces
Accuracy	High for known objects	Varies based on sensor quality
Processing Power	Moderate	High (requires real-time calculations)
Use Cases	Product visualization, museums, training	Indoor navigation, gaming, design

Conclusion

- **Object recognition** enables AR applications to **identify real-world objects** and overlay relevant digital content.

- **Spatial mapping** allows applications to **understand and interact** with the environment, enabling **realistic AR placement**.

- **Combining both techniques** results in powerful AR applications that **recognize objects while understanding their surroundings**.

BY LEVERAGING **ARKit, ARCore, and Vuforia**, developers can create **next-generation AR experiences** that blend **real and digital worlds** seamlessly.

Creating Interactive AR Applications

INTERACTIVE AR APPLICATIONS allow users to engage with digital content in meaningful ways, bridging the gap between the virtual and real worlds. By incorporating user inputs, physics simulations, gestures, voice commands, and AI-driven interactions, AR developers can craft engaging experiences that are both intuitive and immersive.

This section explores key concepts and best practices for building **interactive AR applications**, including **gesture-based interactions, physics simulations, UI/UX considerations, and scripting interactive behaviors** in popular AR development environments.

Understanding Interactivity in AR

INTERACTIVITY IN AR refers to how users engage with virtual elements through:

- **Touch Input**: Users can tap, drag, or resize AR objects.
- **Gestures & Hand Tracking**: Using hand movements to manipulate virtual content.
- **Voice Commands**: Controlling AR objects via speech recognition.
- **Environmental Interactions**: Objects responding to real-world surfaces, lighting, and physics.
- **Multi-User Collaboration**: Enabling shared AR experiences across devices.

Implementing Touch and Gesture Interactions

TOUCH INTERACTIONS are fundamental in **mobile AR applications**. Users should be able to **place, move, scale, and rotate objects** naturally.

Example: Touch-Based Object Manipulation in Unity (C#)

```
USING UNITYENGINE;
using UnityEngine.XR.ARFoundation;
using UnityEngine.XR.ARSubsystems;
public class ARObjectInteraction : MonoBehaviour {
private ARRaycastManager raycastManager;
private GameObject selectedObject;
private Vector2 touchStartPos;
void Start() {
raycastManager = FindObjectOfType<ARRaycastManager>();
}
void Update() {
if (Input.touchCount == 1) {
Touch touch = Input.GetTouch(0);
if (touch.phase == TouchPhase.Began) {
Ray ray = Camera.main.ScreenPointToRay(touch.position);
```

```
RaycastHit hit;

if (Physics.Raycast(ray, out hit)) {

selectedObject = hit.collider.gameObject;

}

}

if (touch.phase == TouchPhase.Moved && selectedObject != null)
{

selectedObject.transform.position += new
Vector3(touch.deltaPosition.x * 0.01f, 0, touch.deltaPosition.y *
0.01f);

}

if (touch.phase == TouchPhase.Ended) {

selectedObject = null;

}

}

}

}
```

This script allows users to **tap on an AR object**, move it by dragging, and release it when done.

Gesture-Based Interactions

GESTURE RECOGNITION in AR enables users to interact with virtual objects **without touching the screen**. SDKs like **ARKit**

(iOS) and ARCore (Android) support **hand tracking and gesture recognition**.

Example: Hand Gesture Detection with ARKit

```
IMPORT ARKIT
import Vision
import UIKit
class ViewController: UIViewController, ARSCNViewDelegate {
@IBOutlet var sceneView: ARSCNView!
private let handPoseRequest = VNDetectHumanHandPoseRequest()
override func viewDidLoad() {
super.viewDidLoad()
sceneView.delegate = self
sceneView.session.run(ARWorldTrackingConfiguration())
}
func captureHandGesture() {
let handler = VNImageRequestHandler(cvPixelBuffer: sceneView.session.currentFrame!.capturedImage, options: [:])
do {
try handler.perform([handPoseRequest])
```

```
if let results = handPoseRequest.results, let observation = results.first {

let recognizedPoints = try observation.recognizedPoints(.all)

if let thumbTip = recognizedPoints[.thumbTip], let indexTip = recognizedPoints[.indexTip] {

let distance = thumbTip.location.distance(to: indexTip.location)

if distance < 0.1 {

print("Pinch gesture detected!")

}

}

}

} catch {

print("Gesture detection failed.")

}

}

}
```

This Swift example detects **pinch gestures**, which can be used to interact with AR objects (e.g., grabbing or resizing them).

Voice Commands in AR

INTEGRATING VOICE COMMANDS allows users to **control AR objects hands-free**. This is useful in **assistive AR applications, smart home control, and accessibility solutions.**

Example: Voice Command-Based Object Manipulation in Unity (C#)

```
USING UNITYENGINE;

using UnityEngine.Windows.Speech;

public class VoiceControlledAR : MonoBehaviour {

private KeywordRecognizer keywordRecognizer;

private Dictionary<string, Action> actions = new Dictionary<string, Action>();

void Start() {

actions.Add("grow", GrowObject);

actions.Add("shrink", ShrinkObject);

keywordRecognizer = new KeywordRecognizer(actions.Keys.ToArray());

keywordRecognizer.OnPhraseRecognized += OnCommandRecognized;

keywordRecognizer.Start();

}

void OnCommandRecognized(PhraseRecognizedEventArgs args) {

if (actions.ContainsKey(args.text)) {

actions[args.text].Invoke();

}
```

```
}
void GrowObject() {
transform.localScale *= 1.2f;
}
void ShrinkObject() {
transform.localScale *= 0.8f;
}
}
```

This Unity script enables **voice recognition** to make AR objects **grow or shrink** based on spoken commands.

Physics-Based Interactions in AR

ADDING **real-world physics** to AR applications makes interactions more **realistic**. This includes:

- **Gravity Simulation**: Objects falling naturally when released.
- **Collisions**: Preventing AR objects from passing through real-world objects.
- **Force Interactions**: Applying physics-based impulses when objects are tapped or thrown.

Example: Adding Physics to an AR Object in Unity

```
USING UNITYENGINE;
```

```
public class ARPhysicsObject : MonoBehaviour {
private Rigidbody rb;
void Start() {
rb = gameObject.AddComponent<Rigidbody>();
rb.useGravity = true;
rb.mass = 1.0f;
}
void OnCollisionEnter(Collision collision) {
Debug.Log("Collided with " + collision.gameObject.name);
}
}
```

This script makes AR objects **fall naturally** due to gravity and **interact with surfaces.**

Multi-User Interactions and Shared AR Experiences

MANY MODERN AR APPLICATIONS allow **multiple users to interact in the same AR space.** This is useful for:

- **Collaborative Workspaces**: Teams working on virtual 3D models.
- **Multiplayer AR Games**: Players interacting in a shared AR environment.
- **Remote Assistance**: Experts guiding users through AR overlays.

Example: Shared AR Experiences with ARKit

USING **Apple's ARKit and Cloud Anchors**, users can **place objects in a shared environment**.

```
import ARKit

import MultipeerConnectivity

class SharedARViewController: UIViewController {

var session = ARSession()

func shareAnchor(anchor: ARAnchor) {

let data = try! NSKeyedArchiver.archivedData(withRootObject: anchor, requiringSecureCoding: true)

sendDataToPeers(data)

}

}
```

This Swift code **shares AR anchors** across devices, allowing users to interact in a **collaborative AR space**.

UI/UX Considerations for Interactive AR

CREATING **intuitive AR interactions** requires careful consideration of user experience. Best practices include:

- **Clear Instructions**: Guide users on how to interact with AR objects.
- **Visual Feedback**: Use animations and highlights to indicate interactive elements.

- **Accessibility Features**: Include voice commands and gesture controls for inclusivity.
- **Natural Interactions**: Align interactions with real-world expectations (e.g., grabbing an object behaves like real life).

Conclusion

- **Interactive AR applications** enhance user engagement by supporting **touch, gestures, voice, and physics-based interactions**.
- **Gesture and voice recognition** improve accessibility and usability in AR applications.
- **Physics simulations** make AR objects behave naturally, increasing realism.
- **Multi-user AR experiences** enable collaborative and social interactions.
- **UI/UX design principles** ensure users can intuitively interact with AR content.

BY LEVERAGING **ARKit, ARCore, Unity, and Vuforia**, developers can create **highly interactive and immersive AR experiences** that are both functional and engaging.

Chapter 5: Developing Virtual Reality Applications

VR SDKs: Oculus, SteamVR, and OpenXR

VIRTUAL REALITY (VR) development relies heavily on specialized software development kits (SDKs) that provide the necessary tools, libraries, and APIs for creating immersive experiences. Among the most widely used VR SDKs are **Oculus SDK**, **SteamVR SDK**, and **OpenXR**. Each of these SDKs has its own strengths, ecosystem, and compatibility considerations. This section explores these SDKs in detail, compares their features, and provides guidance on choosing the right one for your project.

Introduction to VR SDKs

A VR SDK ACTS AS AN interface between the hardware (such as VR headsets and controllers) and the software application. It provides functionalities such as:

- **Rendering VR environments**: Handling stereoscopic rendering, foveated rendering, and optimizations.
- **Tracking user movement**: Providing 6 degrees of freedom (6DOF) tracking for headsets and controllers.
- **Input handling**: Mapping VR controllers, hand tracking, and gesture recognition.
- **Performance optimizations**: Reducing latency, reprojection techniques, and frame rate stabilization.

- **Interfacing with VR platforms**: Enabling deployment to Oculus, SteamVR, or other VR systems.

Oculus SDK

OCULUS (NOW UNDER META) provides a robust ecosystem for VR development, particularly for its own hardware, such as the Meta Quest, Quest 2, and Quest Pro.

Features of Oculus SDK:

- **Oculus Integration for Unity and Unreal Engine**: A set of plugins that extend the default VR capabilities of these engines.
- **Hand Tracking API**: Allows developers to create controller-free interactions.
- **Passthrough API**: Enables mixed reality experiences by blending VR with real-world video feed.
- **Spatial Anchors**: Persistent world-scale tracking for placing virtual objects in the real world.
- **Asynchronous SpaceWarp (ASW) & TimeWarp**: Techniques to improve performance by reducing motion blur and judder.

Setting Up Oculus SDK in Unity

TO DEVELOP A VR APPLICATION using Oculus SDK in Unity:

1. **Install Unity**: Ensure you have the latest version of Unity

with VR support.

2. **Enable XR Plugin Management**: Go to *Edit* > *Project Settings* > *XR Plugin Management* and install the *Oculus XR Plugin*.
3. **Import Oculus Integration Package**: Download the Oculus Integration package from the Unity Asset Store.
4. **Set up VR Camera**: Replace the default camera with an *OVRCameraRig* from the Oculus package.
5. **Configure Input**: Use *OVRInput* for handling controller interactions.

Example code for setting up basic VR movement using Oculus controllers:

```
using UnityEngine;

public class VRMovement : MonoBehaviour

{

public float speed = 3.0f;

void Update()

{

Vector2 joystickInput = OVRInput.Get(OVRInput.Axis2D.PrimaryThumbstick);

transform.position += new Vector3(joystickInput.x, 0, joystickInput.y) * speed * Time.deltaTime;

}

}
```

SteamVR SDK

STEAMVR, DEVELOPED by Valve, is another popular SDK that provides extensive support for multiple VR headsets, including HTC Vive, Valve Index, and even Oculus devices.

Features of SteamVR SDK:

- **Supports multiple VR headsets**: Works across different hardware brands.
- **Lighthouse tracking system**: Enables high-precision room-scale tracking.
- **SteamVR Input System**: Provides a flexible action-based input mapping.
- **Mixed Reality Capture (MRC)**: Allows overlaying real-world video into VR for content creation.
- **OpenVR API**: A cross-platform VR API that can be used independently of SteamVR.

Setting Up SteamVR SDK in Unity

1. **Install SteamVR Plugin**: Download the *SteamVR Plugin* from the Unity Asset Store.
2. **Enable OpenVR**: Go to *Edit* > *Project Settings* > *XR Plugin Management* and enable *OpenVR*.
3. **Add SteamVR Camera Rig**: Drag the *SteamVR Player Prefab* into the scene.
4. **Configure Inputs**: Use the *SteamVR Input System* to map controller actions.

EXAMPLE CODE FOR HANDLING input from a SteamVR controller:

```
using UnityEngine;

using Valve.VR;

public class GrabObject : MonoBehaviour

{

public SteamVR_Input_Sources handType;

public SteamVR_Action_Boolean grabAction;

private GameObject grabbedObject;

void Update()

{

if (grabAction.GetStateDown(handType))

{

// Logic for grabbing an object

}

}

}
```

OpenXR

OPENXR IS AN OPEN STANDARD developed by the Khronos Group that aims to unify VR development across multiple platforms and devices.

Features of OpenXR:

- **Cross-platform compatibility**: Works with Oculus, SteamVR, Windows Mixed Reality, and other platforms.
- **Extensible API**: Allows developers to build future-proof applications.
- **Standardized Input and Rendering**: Reduces dependency on proprietary SDKs.

Setting Up OpenXR in Unity

1. **Enable OpenXR**: Install the *OpenXR Plugin* in Unity's *XR Plugin Management.*
2. **Select Runtime**: Choose the OpenXR runtime for your target device.
3. **Configure Input Actions**: Map interactions using the OpenXR Action System.

EXAMPLE CODE FOR HANDLING OpenXR input:

```
using UnityEngine;

using UnityEngine.InputSystem.XR;

public class OpenXRMovement : MonoBehaviour

{

public InputActionProperty moveAction;

void Update()

{
```

```
Vector2 input = moveAction.action.ReadValue<Vector2>();
transform.position += new Vector3(input.x, 0, input.y) * Time.deltaTime;
}
}
```

Choosing the Right SDK

Feature	Oculus SDK	SteamVR SDK	OpenXR
Platform Support	Oculus Quest, Rift	HTC Vive, Valve Index, Oculus	Cross-platform
Input System	OVRInput	SteamVR Input System	OpenXR Actions
Performance Optimization	ASW, TimeWarp	Reprojection, Motion Smoothing	Vendor-dependent
Mixed Reality Features	Passthrough API	MRC	Partial Support

- **If developing for Meta devices**: Use **Oculus SDK**.
- **If targeting multiple platforms**: Use **OpenXR**.
- **If deploying on SteamVR**: Use **SteamVR SDK**.

Conclusion

UNDERSTANDING THE STRENGTHS and weaknesses of different VR SDKs is crucial for effective VR development. Oculus SDK is best for Meta devices, SteamVR provides strong multi-device support, and OpenXR offers a standardized approach for future-proof VR applications. By selecting the right SDK, developers can ensure optimal performance, flexibility, and compatibility for their VR experiences.

Designing Immersive Virtual Environments

CREATING IMMERSIVE virtual environments is one of the most critical aspects of Virtual Reality (VR) development. Unlike traditional 2D interfaces or even 3D-rendered applications on screens, VR places the user inside the environment, making spatial design, interaction, and realism essential components of a successful experience.

This section explores the fundamental principles of designing immersive virtual environments, including world-building, user experience considerations, environmental realism, interaction mechanics, and performance optimizations.

Principles of Immersive Environment Design

A WELL-DESIGNED VR environment should achieve the following:

- **Presence**: The user should feel like they are inside a real-world space.
- **Scale and Proportion**: Objects and structures should have realistic proportions to maintain immersion.
- **Depth and Perspective**: The use of proper 3D depth cues enhances realism.
- **Interactive Elements**: The world should react to user actions in intuitive ways.

- **Spatial Audio**: Sound should be directional and distance-based to create a more immersive experience.

By implementing these principles effectively, developers can ensure that their virtual environments feel convincing and engaging.

World-Building in VR

WORLD-BUILDING IN VR extends beyond visual aesthetics; it includes designing an entire ecosystem where users interact naturally. There are key elements to consider when designing virtual worlds:

1. Environment Composition

A VIRTUAL WORLD MUST have logical consistency. Every object should serve a purpose, and the layout should be carefully planned.

- **Architectural Considerations**: Buildings, structures, and open spaces should have realistic layouts.

- **Level Design**: Navigation should be intuitive, allowing users to move smoothly.

- **Boundaries**: The world should define physical or invisible boundaries to guide users.

- **Landscapes and Terrain**: Natural environments should feel organic, with hills, rivers, and varied vegetation.

2. Lighting and Atmosphere

LIGHTING IS A CRITICAL factor in VR world-building because it significantly impacts realism and immersion.

- **Dynamic Lighting**: Changing light sources add depth and realism.
- **Shadows and Reflections**: Correct implementation of shadows enhances the user's perception of depth.
- **Fog and Atmospheric Effects**: These effects add realism and scale to large environments.

Example of setting up dynamic lighting in Unity:

```
using UnityEngine;

public class DynamicLighting : MonoBehaviour

{

public Light directionalLight;

public float daySpeed = 1f;

void Update()

{

directionalLight.transform.Rotate(Vector3.right * daySpeed * Time.deltaTime);

}

}
```

Interaction Mechanics in Virtual Environments

INTERACTION IS A CRUCIAL component of immersion in VR. Without interactivity, even the most detailed worlds can feel static and lifeless.

1. Object Interaction

USERS SHOULD BE ABLE to grab, manipulate, and interact with objects naturally.

- **Physics-Based Interactions**: Objects should respond to real-world physics.
- **Haptic Feedback**: Controllers should provide feedback when interacting with objects.
- **Hand Tracking**: Allowing users to use their hands instead of controllers enhances realism.

Example of basic object grabbing in Unity using XR Interaction Toolkit:

```
using UnityEngine;

using UnityEngine.XR.Interaction.Toolkit;

public class GrabObject : MonoBehaviour

{

public XRGrabInteractable interactable;

void Start()

{
```

```
interactable = GetComponent<XRGrabInteractable>();
}
}
```

2. Navigation in VR

USERS NEED AN EFFECTIVE way to move around large virtual environments. The two main methods are:

- **Teleportation**: A common method where users point to a location and instantly move there.
- **Smooth Locomotion**: Allows continuous movement using controller inputs but can cause motion sickness if not handled properly.

Example of teleportation setup in Unity:

```
using UnityEngine;
using UnityEngine.XR.Interaction.Toolkit;
public class TeleportationSetup : MonoBehaviour
{
public TeleportationProvider teleportProvider;
public Transform targetPosition;
void Update()
{
if (Input.GetKeyDown(KeyCode.T))
```

```
{
TeleportRequest request = new TeleportRequest() { destinationPosition = targetPosition.position };
teleportProvider.QueueTeleportRequest(request);
}
}
}
```

Enhancing Realism in VR Environments

BEYOND BASIC DESIGN, creating a truly immersive world requires additional considerations:

1. Environmental Sound Design

SPATIAL AUDIO PLAYS a crucial role in how users perceive the virtual world.

- **3D Positional Audio**: Ensures sound originates from the correct direction.
- **Reverb and Echo Effects**: Adds realism to indoor and outdoor environments.
- **Adaptive Audio**: Changes based on user actions and environmental events.

Example of setting up 3D audio in Unity:

```
using UnityEngine;
```

```
public class SpatialAudio : MonoBehaviour
{
public AudioSource audioSource;
void Start()
{
audioSource.spatialBlend = 1.0f; // Ensures 3D spatial audio is enabled.
}
}
```

2. AI and NPC Behaviors

TO MAKE A VIRTUAL WORLD feel alive, it should include non-player characters (NPCs) with intelligent behaviors.

- **Pathfinding AI**: Allows NPCs to navigate complex environments.
- **Procedural Behaviors**: NPCs should respond dynamically to user actions.
- **Voice Interaction**: Users should be able to talk to and receive responses from NPCs.

Example of simple AI movement in Unity:

```
using UnityEngine;
using UnityEngine.AI;
```

```
public class NPCMovement : MonoBehaviour
{
public Transform target;
private NavMeshAgent agent;
void Start()
{
agent = GetComponent<NavMeshAgent>();
agent.SetDestination(target.position);
}
}
```

Performance Optimization for VR Environments

VR REQUIRES HIGH FRAME rates (typically 90 FPS or higher) to avoid motion sickness. Here are some key optimization techniques:

1. Reducing Draw Calls

MINIMIZING THE NUMBER of objects rendered at once can significantly improve performance.

- **Batching and Instancing**: Reduces the number of draw calls.
- **Occlusion Culling**: Hides objects that are not in view.

2. Level of Detail (LOD)

USING LOD TECHNIQUES ensures that only high-detail models are rendered close to the user.

Example of LOD setup in Unity:

```
using UnityEngine;

public class LODSetup : MonoBehaviour

{

public LODGroup lodGroup;

void Start()

{

lodGroup = GetComponent<LODGroup>();

}

}
```

3. Asynchronous TimeWarp (ATW) and SpaceWarp

MANY VR PLATFORMS OFFER built-in performance-enhancing technologies:

- **ATW**: Predicts user head movements to reduce latency.
- **SpaceWarp**: Generates synthetic frames when rendering performance drops.

Best Practices for VR Environment Design

TO ENSURE AN OPTIMAL VR experience, follow these best practices:

- **Use Natural Movement and Scale**: Keep world proportions realistic.
- **Optimize for Comfort**: Reduce motion sickness by using stable camera movements.
- **Maintain High Frame Rates**: Ensure the environment runs at a minimum of 90 FPS.
- **Prioritize Accessibility**: Make controls and interactions intuitive for all users.
- **Test in Real Hardware**: Regularly test on VR headsets to identify potential issues.

Conclusion

DESIGNING IMMERSIVE VR environments requires careful attention to spatial design, user interactions, realism, and performance optimizations. By following world-building principles, enhancing interactions, incorporating realistic audio and AI behaviors, and optimizing performance, developers can create engaging and lifelike virtual experiences that keep users fully immersed.

Implementing 6DOF Movement and Controllers

SIX DEGREES OF FREEDOM (6DOF) movement is a crucial aspect of virtual reality (VR), enabling users to interact naturally within a virtual environment. Unlike 3DOF, which limits movement to rotation around three axes (yaw, pitch, and roll), 6DOF includes translational movement (moving forward/backward, left/right, and up/down). This allows for a fully immersive experience, where users can walk, crouch, and reach within a virtual world.

This section covers the fundamental concepts of 6DOF movement, how to implement it using VR SDKs, handling controllers for user interaction, and optimizing movement mechanics for comfort and immersion.

Understanding 6DOF Movement

6DOF MOVEMENT CONSISTS of:

1. **Three rotational movements (angular motion)**

   ○ **Yaw (Horizontal rotation)** – Looking left and right.

   ○ **Pitch (Vertical rotation)** – Looking up and down.

   ○ **Roll (Tilt rotation)** – Tilting the head sideways.

2. **Three translational movements (positional motion)**

   ○ **X-axis (Side-to-side)** – Moving left and right.

   ○ **Y-axis (Vertical movement)** – Moving up and down.

   ○ **Z-axis (Forward and backward)** – Moving closer or farther.

These movements are tracked using sensors in VR headsets and controllers, such as accelerometers, gyroscopes, and external cameras (inside-out tracking) or external base stations (outside-in tracking).

Implementing 6DOF Head Movement

MODERN VR SDKS HANDLE 6DOF tracking for headsets automatically, but it's essential to ensure the camera setup correctly reflects real-world movement.

Setting Up 6DOF in Unity

IN UNITY, USING XR Interaction Toolkit:

1. **Install XR Plugin Management**

   ○ *Edit > Project Settings > XR Plugin Management* and enable the VR platform.

2. **Add an XR Rig**

   ○ The *XR Rig* prefab ensures that the camera follows head movement.

3. **Configure Head Tracking**

   ○ The **XR Camera** automatically tracks movement.

Example code to manually adjust camera position based on headset tracking:

```
using UnityEngine;

using UnityEngine.XR;

public class HeadTracking : MonoBehaviour

{

public Transform cameraTransform;
```

```
void Update()

{

Vector3 headsetPosition = InputTracking.GetLocalPosition(XRNode.Head);

transform.position = headsetPosition;

}

}
```

Implementing 6DOF Locomotion

VR LOCOMOTION ALLOWS users to move beyond their physical play space. There are several techniques for smooth and comfortable locomotion.

1. Smooth Locomotion (Joystick-Based Movement)

THIS METHOD ALLOWS continuous movement using a controller's joystick.

Example implementation:

```
using UnityEngine;

public class SmoothLocomotion : MonoBehaviour

{

public float speed = 2.0f;

public Transform vrCamera;

private CharacterController characterController;
```

```
void Start()

{

characterController = GetComponent<CharacterController>();

}

void Update()

{

Vector3 forward = vrCamera.forward;

forward.y = 0; // Prevent vertical movement

Vector3 move = forward * Input.GetAxis("Vertical") + vrCamera.right * Input.GetAxis("Horizontal");

characterController.Move(move * speed * Time.deltaTime);

}

}
```

2. Teleportation Locomotion (Comfortable Movement)

TELEPORTATION REDUCES motion sickness by allowing users to move instantly to a location.

Steps:

- Enable XR Interaction Toolkit in Unity.
- Add **XR Ray Interactor** to the VR controllers.
- Assign a **Teleportation Provider**.

Example of setting up teleportation in Unity:

```
using UnityEngine;

using UnityEngine.XR.Interaction.Toolkit;

public class Teleport : MonoBehaviour

{

public TeleportationProvider teleportationProvider;

public Transform targetLocation;

void Update()

{

if (Input.GetButtonDown("Fire1"))

{

TeleportRequest request = new TeleportRequest() { destinationPosition = targetLocation.position };

teleportationProvider.QueueTeleportRequest(request);

}

}

}
```

3. Arm-Swing Locomotion (Natural Walking Simulation)

THIS METHOD SIMULATES walking by detecting hand movements.

Example implementation:

```
using UnityEngine;

public class ArmSwingLocomotion : MonoBehaviour

{

public Transform leftController;

public Transform rightController;

public float speed = 3.0f;

void Update()

{

float movement = (leftController.localPosition.z - rightController.localPosition.z) * speed;

transform.position += transform.forward * movement * Time.deltaTime;

}

}
```

Controller Implementation for 6DOF

CONTROLLERS IN VR ARE essential for interaction. They provide **positional tracking**, **button input**, and **gesture recognition**.

1. Mapping Controller Input

EACH VR SDK HAS A UNIQUE way of mapping controller buttons. In Unity, **XR Input System** is used.

Example of detecting button presses:

```
using UnityEngine;

using UnityEngine.XR;

public class VRControllerInput : MonoBehaviour

{

public XRNode controllerNode;

private InputDevice controller;

void Start()

{

controller = InputDevices.GetDeviceAtXRNode(controllerNode);

}

void Update()

{

if (controller.TryGetFeatureValue(CommonUsages.primaryButton, out bool isPressed) && isPressed)

{

Debug.Log("Primary button pressed");

}
```

```
}
}
```

2. Object Interaction with Controllers

USERS SHOULD BE ABLE to grab and manipulate objects.

Steps:

- Add an **XR Grab Interactable** to objects.
- Assign **XR Ray Interactor** for remote grabbing.

Example implementation:

```
using UnityEngine;
using UnityEngine.XR.Interaction.Toolkit;
public class VRGrab : MonoBehaviour
{
public XRGrabInteractable grabInteractable;
void Start()
{
grabInteractable = GetComponent<XRGrabInteractable>();
}
}
```

Optimizing 6DOF Movement for Comfort

WHILE 6DOF MOVEMENT enhances immersion, poorly designed locomotion can cause **motion sickness**. Here are key optimization techniques:

1. Reduce Acceleration and Deceleration

- Sudden stops and fast movements should be avoided.
- Use gradual acceleration.

2. Implement VR Comfort Mode

- Add a vignette effect when moving.
- Reduce field of view dynamically.

3. Snap Turning Instead of Smooth Turning

- Gradually turning the camera causes discomfort.
- Snap turning moves the user in fixed increments.

EXAMPLE OF SNAP TURNING:

```
using UnityEngine;

public class SnapTurn : MonoBehaviour

{

public float turnAngle = 30f;

void Update()
```

```
{
if (Input.GetKeyDown(KeyCode.RightArrow))
transform.Rotate(Vector3.up, turnAngle);
else if (Input.GetKeyDown(KeyCode.LeftArrow))
transform.Rotate(Vector3.up, -turnAngle);
}
}
```

4. Maintain High Frame Rates

- VR applications should run at **90 FPS or higher**.
- Reduce polygon count and optimize shaders.

Best Practices for 6DOF Implementation

- **Use natural motion mechanics**: Avoid artificial movement when possible.
- **Allow user customization**: Different users have different tolerances.
- **Balance interactivity with comfort**: Not all users can handle intense movement.
- **Test with real users**: Playtesting is essential to find comfort issues.

Conclusion

IMPLEMENTING 6DOF MOVEMENT in VR requires a balance between realism, interactivity, and user comfort. By leveraging proper locomotion techniques, optimizing controller interactions, and maintaining high performance, developers can create fluid and immersive VR experiences.

Best Practices for Comfort and Motion Sickness Reduction

VIRTUAL REALITY (VR) has the potential to provide highly immersive experiences, but if not designed properly, it can lead to **motion sickness**, **discomfort**, and **fatigue**. A poorly optimized VR experience can cause users to feel **dizzy, nauseated, or disoriented**, leading to a lack of engagement and potential health risks.

This section explores the causes of motion sickness in VR, best practices for comfort, effective design techniques, locomotion optimizations, and real-world implementation strategies to ensure a comfortable and accessible VR experience.

Understanding Motion Sickness in VR

MOTION SICKNESS IN VR, also called **virtual reality sickness**, occurs when there is a **disconnect between the user's sensory inputs**. The three primary factors causing motion sickness are:

1. **Sensory Conflict**: The brain receives mismatched signals from the eyes (visual motion) and inner ear (physical motion), leading to discomfort.
2. **Latency and Jitter**: Delays in tracking movement or rendering frames cause unnatural motion, which confuses the brain.

3. **Inconsistent Frame Rate**: A VR experience must maintain a **high and stable frame rate (90 FPS or above)** to prevent stuttering and lag.

Other contributing factors include **field of view (FOV), movement speed, acceleration**, and **user sensitivity**.

Best Practices for Reducing Motion Sickness

1. Maintain a High Frame Rate (90+ FPS)

A LOW FRAME RATE (<60 FPS) increases **latency** and causes stuttering, which directly contributes to nausea. The ideal VR experience should run at **90 FPS or higher** for a smooth and responsive feel.

Optimization Techniques:

- **Reduce polygon count**: Optimize 3D models and textures to reduce GPU load.
- **Use occlusion culling**: Hide objects not visible to the player to improve performance.
- **Implement Level of Detail (LOD)**: Load lower-quality assets when objects are distant.

EXAMPLE OF LOD IMPLEMENTATION in Unity:

```
using UnityEngine;

public class LODSetup : MonoBehaviour

{
```

```
public LODGroup lodGroup;
void Start()
{
lodGroup = GetComponent<LODGroup>();
}
}
```

2. Reduce Latency with Predictive Tracking

LATENCY SHOULD BE BELOW **20 milliseconds** to avoid noticeable delays. One approach is to use **predictive tracking**, where the VR system estimates the player's movement ahead of time.

Techniques to Reduce Latency:

- **Use Asynchronous SpaceWarp (ASW) and TimeWarp** (on Oculus headsets).
- **Enable Motion Smoothing** in SteamVR for improved frame interpolation.
- **Optimize rendering pipelines** to prevent bottlenecks.

EXAMPLE OF ENABLING Oculus SpaceWarp:

```
OVRManager.fixedFoveatedRenderingLevel =
OVRManager.FixedFoveatedRenderingLevel.High;
```

3. Use a Comfortable Field of View (FOV)

A WIDE **field of view (FOV)** can increase immersion but also intensify motion sickness. A sudden **FOV change** can be disorienting, so gradual shifts should be used.

Recommended FOV Adjustments:

- **Restrict FOV dynamically** during movement to reduce nausea.
- **Avoid excessive zooming** and sudden FOV changes.
- **Provide user-adjustable FOV settings.**

EXAMPLE OF ADJUSTING FOV dynamically in Unity:

```
using UnityEngine;

public class DynamicFOV : MonoBehaviour

{

public Camera vrCamera;

public float normalFOV = 90f;

public float reducedFOV = 70f;

void Update()

{

if (Input.GetKey(KeyCode.W)) // Reduce FOV while moving

vrCamera.fieldOfView = reducedFOV;
```

```
else
vrCamera.fieldOfView = normalFOV;
}
}
```

---

4. Implement Natural Locomotion Techniques

ONE OF THE BIGGEST causes of VR sickness is **artificial movement**, which occurs when the user is stationary but moves within the virtual world.

Recommended Locomotion Techniques:

1. **Teleportation** – Jumping instantly to locations instead of smooth movement.
2. **Arm Swing Locomotion** – Moving by swinging the arms naturally.
3. **Smooth Movement (With Comfort Options)** – For experienced VR users, slow movement with **vignette effects** can help reduce discomfort.

EXAMPLE OF TELEPORTATION:

```
using UnityEngine;
using UnityEngine.XR.Interaction.Toolkit;
public class Teleport : MonoBehaviour
{
public TeleportationProvider teleportationProvider;
```

```
public Transform targetLocation;

void Update()

{

if (Input.GetButtonDown("Fire1"))

{

TeleportRequest request = new TeleportRequest() { destinationPosition = targetLocation.position };

teleportationProvider.QueueTeleportRequest(request);

}

}

}
```

5. Use Snap Turning Instead of Smooth Turning

SMOOTH ROTATION in VR can be highly uncomfortable. Instead, **snap turning** (rotating in fixed increments) reduces disorientation.

Example of snap turning:

```
using UnityEngine;

public class SnapTurn : MonoBehaviour

{

public float turnAngle = 30f;

void Update()
```

```
{
if (Input.GetKeyDown(KeyCode.RightArrow))
transform.Rotate(Vector3.up, turnAngle);
else if (Input.GetKeyDown(KeyCode.LeftArrow))
transform.Rotate(Vector3.up, -turnAngle);
}
}
```

6. Provide Visual Stabilization

VR ENVIRONMENTS SHOULD include **fixed reference points** to reduce visual confusion.

Recommended Stabilization Methods:

- **Cockpit View** – Adding a static frame of reference (used in racing games).
- **Vignette Effect** – Reducing peripheral vision during movement.
- **Head-Based Motion Prediction** – Adjusting camera movement based on user input.

EXAMPLE OF VIGNETTE effect:

```
using UnityEngine;
public class VignetteEffect : MonoBehaviour
```

```
{
public Material vignetteMaterial;
private float intensity = 0f;
void Update()
{
if (Input.GetKey(KeyCode.W)) // Apply vignette when moving
intensity = Mathf.Lerp(intensity, 0.5f, Time.deltaTime * 2);
else
intensity = Mathf.Lerp(intensity, 0f, Time.deltaTime * 2);
vignetteMaterial.SetFloat("_VignetteIntensity", intensity);
}
}
```

7. Optimize Interaction Timing

POOR TIMING IN INTERACTIONS (e.g., button presses, grabbing objects) can increase disorientation.

Best Practices for Interaction:

- **Use haptic feedback** to provide real-time responses.
- **Delay actions appropriately** (avoid instant interactions).
- **Ensure physics-based interactions feel natural**.

EXAMPLE OF ADDING HAPTIC feedback:

```
using UnityEngine;

using UnityEngine.XR;

public class HapticFeedback : MonoBehaviour

{

public XRNode controllerNode;

private InputDevice controller;

void Start()

{

controller = InputDevices.GetDeviceAtXRNode(controllerNode);

}

public void TriggerHapticPulse(float duration, float strength)

{

controller.SendHapticImpulse(0, strength, duration);

}

}
```

Best Practices Summary

Factor	Best Practice
Frame Rate	Maintain **90+ FPS** for smooth visuals.
Latency	Keep below **20ms** for reduced delay.
FOV	Avoid sudden **FOV changes**, allow customization.
Locomotion	Use **teleportation or arm-swing** movement for comfort.
Rotation	Prefer **snap turning** over smooth turning.
Visual Stability	Add **vignette effects** and **cockpit view** for reference.
Haptic Feedback	Use **controller vibrations** for interactions.

Conclusion

MOTION SICKNESS IN VR can be **mitigated through proper design choices**, including **high frame rates, optimized locomotion techniques, stabilized visuals, and predictive tracking**. By implementing best practices, developers can create VR experiences that **maximize immersion while minimizing discomfort**, ensuring that users of all experience levels can enjoy virtual reality comfortably.

Chapter 6: Advanced AR & VR Development Techniques

AI and Machine Learning in AR & VR

ARTIFICIAL INTELLIGENCE (AI) and Machine Learning (ML) are transforming the landscape of Augmented Reality (AR) and Virtual Reality (VR). By integrating AI-driven algorithms, AR & VR applications can become more intelligent, adaptive, and immersive. This section explores various applications of AI in AR & VR, key machine learning techniques, and practical implementations.

The Role of AI in AR & VR

AI ENHANCES AR & VR experiences by making virtual environments more interactive and responsive. Some of the major areas where AI is utilized in AR & VR include:

1. **Computer Vision** – AI-driven image recognition enables AR systems to detect and track real-world objects, surfaces, and environments with high accuracy.
2. **Natural Language Processing (NLP)** – AI-powered voice assistants allow users to interact with AR & VR applications using voice commands.
3. **Gesture Recognition** – AI models can interpret hand movements and facial expressions to provide more natural interactions.
4. **Behavioral Prediction** – AI can analyze user actions and predict their next moves to create personalized experiences.
5. **Procedural Content Generation** – AI can dynamically generate virtual environments, reducing the need for

extensive manual design.

6. **Real-time Adaptation** – AI-powered AR & VR systems can adjust in real time based on user behavior, environmental conditions, and device capabilities.

Machine Learning Techniques for AR & VR

SEVERAL MACHINE LEARNING techniques contribute to enhancing AR & VR applications. Below are some of the most important ones:

1. Computer Vision and Image Recognition

COMPUTER VISION IS fundamental for AR applications that need to recognize and augment objects in the real world. Convolutional Neural Networks (CNNs) are commonly used for:

- Object detection
- Scene understanding
- Face tracking
- Markerless AR tracking

Example: Using OpenCV and TensorFlow for object recognition in AR:

```
import cv2

import tensorflow as tf

import numpy as np

# Load a pre-trained deep learning model
```

```
model =
tf.keras.models.load_model("object_recognition_model.h5")

# Capture a frame from the camera

cap = cv2.VideoCapture(0)

while True:

ret, frame = cap.read()

if not ret:

break

# Preprocess the frame

resized_frame = cv2.resize(frame, (224, 224))

normalized_frame = resized_frame / 255.0

input_frame = np.expand_dims(normalized_frame, axis=0)

# Predict objects

predictions = model.predict(input_frame)

print("Detected Object:", predictions)

cv2.imshow("AR Object Recognition", frame)

if cv2.waitKey(1) & 0xFF == ord('q'):

break

cap.release()

cv2.destroyAllWindows()
```

2. Reinforcement Learning for Adaptive AR/VR Experiences

REINFORCEMENT LEARNING (RL) is used to train AI agents to learn from their environment. This is particularly useful in VR gaming and simulations where an AI character needs to adapt to the user's actions.

- AI-driven NPCs (Non-Playable Characters) in VR can learn and react dynamically.
- AR training simulations can adjust difficulty based on the user's skill level.

Example: Using OpenAI Gym for reinforcement learning in a VR simulation:

```
import gym

# Create an RL environment

env = gym.make("CartPole-v1")

state = env.reset()

for _ in range(1000):

action = env.action_space.sample() # Random action

state, reward, done, _ = env.step(action)

env.render()

if done:

state = env.reset()

env.close()
```

3. Generative Adversarial Networks (GANs) for Realistic Content Generation

GANS ARE WIDELY USED in AR & VR to create realistic textures, environments, and even synthetic human models. GANs can:

- Enhance AR object textures to make them more photorealistic.
- Generate lifelike VR characters.
- Create AI-driven facial animations.

Example: Generating realistic AR textures using a GAN model in Python:

```
from tensorflow.keras.models import Sequential

from tensorflow.keras.layers import Dense, Reshape, Conv2DTranspose

import numpy as np

# Simple GAN Generator model

generator = Sequential([

Dense(128, activation='relu', input_shape=(100,)),

Dense(256, activation='relu'),

Dense(512, activation='relu'),

Dense(1024, activation='relu'),

Dense(64 * 64 * 3, activation='tanh'),
```

```
Reshape((64, 64, 3))

])

# Generate a synthetic AR texture

noise = np.random.normal(0, 1, (1, 100))

synthetic_texture = generator.predict(noise)
```

AI-Powered Voice and Gesture Control in AR & VR

ONE OF THE MOST PROMISING applications of AI in AR & VR is the ability to interact with digital environments using voice and gestures.

1. Voice Control with AI

SPEECH RECOGNITION enables users to control AR & VR applications hands-free. AI-powered voice assistants like Google Assistant and Siri are being integrated into AR & VR platforms.

Example: Using Google's Speech-to-Text API for voice commands in AR:

```
import speech_recognition as sr

recognizer = sr.Recognizer()

with sr.Microphone() as source:

print("Say something...")

audio = recognizer.listen(source)

try:
```

```
text = recognizer.recognize_google(audio)

print("You said:", text)

except sr.UnknownValueError:

print("Sorry, could not understand audio")

except sr.RequestError:

print("Error with speech recognition service")
```

2. Gesture Recognition with AI

GESTURE-BASED INTERACTION is crucial for intuitive AR & VR experiences. AI models trained with deep learning can recognize hand movements and translate them into commands.

Example: Hand tracking using MediaPipe:

```
import cv2

import mediapipe as mp

mp_hands = mp.solutions.hands

hands = mp_hands.Hands()

cap = cv2.VideoCapture(0)

while cap.isOpened():

ret, frame = cap.read()

if not ret:

break
```

```
frame_rgb = cv2.cvtColor(frame, cv2.COLOR_BGR2RGB)
results = hands.process(frame_rgb)
if results.multi_hand_landmarks:
for hand_landmarks in results.multi_hand_landmarks:
print("Hand landmarks detected")
cv2.imshow("Hand Tracking", frame)
if cv2.waitKey(1) & 0xFF == ord('q'):
break
cap.release()
cv2.destroyAllWindows()
```

Real-World Use Cases of AI in AR & VR

AI-DRIVEN AR & VR APPLICATIONS are being used across various industries:

1. **Healthcare** – AI-powered AR applications assist in surgeries by overlaying real-time patient data.
2. **Retail** – Virtual try-on solutions use AI to enhance AR shopping experiences.
3. **Education** – AI-driven VR tutors provide personalized learning.
4. **Gaming** – AI NPCs in VR adapt to player behaviors.
5. **Automotive** – AI-enhanced AR HUDs (Head-Up Displays) provide drivers with real-time navigation.

Conclusion

AI AND MACHINE LEARNING are rapidly advancing the capabilities of AR & VR applications. With computer vision, reinforcement learning, GANs, and natural interaction models, AI is making AR & VR experiences smarter and more immersive. As technology evolves, AI will continue to play a critical role in shaping the future of AR & VR applications.

Cloud Computing and Edge Processing in AR & VR

CLOUD COMPUTING AND edge processing have revolutionized the way Augmented Reality (AR) and Virtual Reality (VR) applications function. These technologies enable complex computations to be offloaded to powerful cloud servers or processed at the network's edge, leading to enhanced performance, reduced latency, and improved user experiences. This section explores how cloud computing and edge processing optimize AR & VR applications, the technologies involved, real-world applications, and best practices for implementation.

The Need for Cloud Computing and Edge Processing in AR & VR

AR & VR APPLICATIONS require immense processing power due to their reliance on real-time rendering, AI-driven interactions, and large datasets. Traditional local processing often leads to:

- High latency, causing motion sickness and reducing immersion.
- Performance bottlenecks on resource-limited devices.

- Increased battery consumption in mobile AR/VR devices.
- Limited scalability for multi-user experiences.

Cloud computing and edge processing address these challenges by distributing computational workloads between cloud servers and edge devices, ensuring efficient data processing and real-time responses.

Cloud Computing for AR & VR

CLOUD COMPUTING LEVERAGES remote data centers to process AR & VR workloads, enabling applications to run on devices with limited computational power. Some of the key benefits include:

1. **High Performance** – Cloud servers can perform complex tasks such as AI-based object recognition and real-time physics simulations.
2. **Scalability** – Cloud-based AR & VR applications can handle multiple users simultaneously without device limitations.
3. **Reduced Device Load** – By offloading computations to the cloud, AR/VR headsets and mobile devices experience improved performance and battery life.
4. **Data Storage and Synchronization** – Cloud storage enables seamless cross-device synchronization and real-time updates.

Cloud-Based Rendering

CLOUD-BASED RENDERING, also known as "cloud gaming" in the VR space, allows rendering-heavy computations to be performed on cloud servers, streaming high-quality visuals to lightweight VR headsets or AR glasses.

Example of using a cloud rendering service in Unity:

```
using UnityEngine;

using System.Collections;

public class CloudRendering : MonoBehaviour

{

private string cloudRenderingServerUrl = "https://your-cloud-server.com/render";

IEnumerator Start()

{

WWW request = new WWW(cloudRenderingServerUrl);

yield return request;

if (request.error == null)

{

Texture2D renderedTexture = new Texture2D(2, 2);

renderedTexture.LoadImage(request.bytes);

GetComponent<Renderer>().material.mainTexture = renderedTexture;

}

}
```

```
}
```

Edge Processing in AR & VR

EDGE PROCESSING, ALSO known as edge computing, brings computation closer to the end-user by utilizing edge devices such as AR headsets, 5G edge nodes, or on-premise servers. Unlike cloud computing, which relies on remote data centers, edge processing reduces latency by executing critical computations closer to the user.

Benefits of Edge Processing in AR & VR

1. **Ultra-Low Latency** – Processes critical tasks in milliseconds, crucial for real-time AR/VR applications.
2. **Improved Privacy** – Sensitive data can be processed locally instead of being sent to the cloud.
3. **Reduced Bandwidth Usage** – Minimizes the need to send large data packets to remote servers.
4. **Offline Functionality** – AR & VR applications remain functional even without an internet connection.

Example of Edge AI for Object Detection in AR

BY LEVERAGING EDGE AI models, AR applications can recognize objects locally without cloud dependency:

```
import cv2

import tensorflow.lite as tflite

# Load Edge AI model

interpreter =
tflite.Interpreter(model_path="edge_object_detection.tflite")
```

```
interpreter.allocate_tensors()

cap = cv2.VideoCapture(0)

while cap.isOpened():

ret, frame = cap.read()

if not ret:

break

# Preprocess frame for AI model

resized_frame = cv2.resize(frame, (224, 224))

input_data = resized_frame / 255.0

input_data = input_data.reshape(1, 224, 224, 3)

# Perform inference on the edge device

interpreter.set_tensor(interpreter.get_input_details()[0]['index'],
input_data)

interpreter.invoke()

output_data =
interpreter.get_tensor(interpreter.get_output_details()[0]['index'])

print("Detected Object:", output_data)

cv2.imshow("Edge AI AR", frame)

if cv2.waitKey(1) & 0xFF == ord('q'):

break

cap.release()
```

cv2.destroyAllWindows()

Cloud vs. Edge Computing: Choosing the Right Approach

THE CHOICE BETWEEN cloud and edge computing depends on various factors such as application requirements, network conditions, and processing needs.

Factor	Cloud Computing	Edge Computing
Latency	Higher due to network dependency	Lower, real-time responses
Computational Power	High, capable of running complex AI models	Limited to local device capabilities
Bandwidth Usage	Requires internet bandwidth	Operates with minimal network dependency
Scalability	Highly scalable for multi-user applications	Limited to available edge devices
Offline Capability	Requires internet connectivity	Works even in offline mode

Hybrid solutions often combine both approaches, using edge computing for real-time interactions and cloud computing for storage and AI model updates.

5G and Its Role in Cloud & Edge AR/VR

THE ADVENT OF **5G technology** has significantly boosted the efficiency of cloud and edge processing for AR & VR applications. Key benefits include:

1. **Ultra-Fast Data Transmission** – Supports real-time rendering and multi-user VR.
2. **Low Latency** – Reduces input lag in AR applications.

3. **Edge-Optimized Processing** – Enables AI computations closer to the user.

Example: Streaming AR content using 5G and edge processing:

```
navigator.connection.addEventListener('change', () => {

if (navigator.connection.effectiveType === '5g') {

console.log('5G connection detected, switching to high-quality AR streaming mode.');

// Load high-resolution AR assets

}

});
```

Cloud & Edge Security Considerations for AR & VR

SECURITY IS A MAJOR concern when handling real-time data in AR & VR environments. Implementing proper security measures ensures user privacy and protects data from cyber threats.

Security Best Practices:

1. **Data Encryption** – Encrypt AR/VR data during transmission and storage.
2. **Access Control** – Implement multi-factor authentication for cloud-based AR/VR applications.
3. **Edge AI Privacy** – Ensure on-device AI models do not store user data without permission.
4. **Secure APIs** – Use OAuth2 and API gateways to protect cloud-based AR services.

EXAMPLE OF IMPLEMENTING secure authentication in a cloud-based AR system:

```
from flask import Flask, request, jsonify

import jwt

app = Flask(__name__)

SECRET_KEY = "your_secret_key"

@app.route('/authenticate', methods=['POST'])

def authenticate():

data = request.json

if data['username'] == "user" and data['password'] == "securepassword":

token = jwt.encode({'user': data['username']}, SECRET_KEY, algorithm="HS256")

return jsonify({"token": token})

return jsonify({"error": "Invalid credentials"}), 401

if __name__ == '__main__':

app.run()
```

Future Trends in Cloud & Edge AR/VR

1. **AI-Powered Edge Devices** – Future AR/VR devices will have built-in AI chips for local processing.
2. **Quantum Computing in AR/VR** – Quantum cloud computing may revolutionize rendering speeds.
3. **Decentralized AR/VR Networks** – Blockchain and

decentralized computing may reduce reliance on cloud servers.

4. **Holographic Streaming** – Cloud-powered holographic AR will enable more realistic experiences.

Conclusion

CLOUD COMPUTING AND edge processing have redefined the capabilities of AR & VR applications by enhancing performance, reducing latency, and enabling large-scale interactions. By leveraging a hybrid approach, developers can create more efficient, scalable, and immersive AR & VR experiences. As technology evolves, 5G, AI-driven edge computing, and security advancements will further propel the future of AR & VR applications.

Networking and Multi-User AR & VR Experiences

NETWORKING AND MULTI-user interactions are essential for creating immersive AR & VR experiences that allow users to collaborate, socialize, and interact in shared virtual spaces. Multi-user AR & VR environments leverage real-time networking to synchronize actions, positions, and events across different devices, creating a cohesive and interactive experience.

This section explores the fundamental concepts of networking in AR & VR, real-time synchronization techniques, cloud-based multiplayer architectures, and best practices for developing multi-user applications.

Importance of Networking in AR & VR

MULTI-USER EXPERIENCES in AR & VR require seamless communication between devices to maintain immersion and interaction fidelity. Some of the major use cases include:

1. **Social VR** – Platforms like Meta Horizon Worlds allow users to engage with others in virtual spaces.
2. **Collaborative AR** – AR applications like Microsoft HoloLens enable teams to collaborate on 3D models.
3. **Multiplayer Gaming** – VR multiplayer games require real-time synchronization of player actions.
4. **Training Simulations** – Military and medical training simulations benefit from synchronized multi-user VR environments.

To achieve a smooth networking experience, AR & VR applications rely on various networking architectures and protocols.

Networking Architectures for AR & VR

1. Peer-to-Peer (P2P) Networking

P2P NETWORKING ALLOWS AR & VR devices to communicate directly without relying on a central server. This approach is useful for small-scale applications where latency is a critical factor.

Advantages:

- Low latency due to direct communication.
- Reduces server costs.

- Ideal for local multiplayer AR experiences.

Disadvantages:

- Difficult to scale for large applications.
- Network stability depends on peer availability.

Example: Establishing a simple WebRTC P2P connection for AR collaboration:

```
const peerConnection = new RTCPeerConnection();

navigator.mediaDevices.getUserMedia({ video: true, audio: true })

.then(stream => {

peerConnection.addStream(stream);

});

peerConnection.onicecandidate = event => {

if (event.candidate) {

sendCandidateToPeer(event.candidate);

}

};
```

2. Client-Server Model

IN A CLIENT-SERVER model, all AR & VR devices connect to a centralized server that manages the synchronization of data, interactions, and player movements.

Advantages:

- Easier to scale for large multi-user environments.
- Centralized authority ensures consistency and security.
- Supports persistent AR experiences.

Disadvantages:

- Higher latency compared to P2P.
- Requires dedicated server infrastructure.

Example: Using Node.js with WebSockets for a multi-user AR/VR server:

```
const WebSocket = require('ws');
const wss = new WebSocket.Server({ port: 8080 });
wss.on('connection', ws => {
ws.on('message', message => {
console.log(`Received: ${message}`);
wss.clients.forEach(client => {
if (client !== ws && client.readyState === WebSocket.OPEN) {
client.send(message);
}
});
});
```

```
});
```

3. Cloud-Based Multiplayer Networking

CLOUD-BASED MULTIPLAYER networking uses cloud infrastructure to manage multi-user interactions in real time. Services like AWS GameLift, Google Cloud Game Servers, and Firebase provide scalable solutions.

Advantages:

- Auto-scaling capabilities for large user bases.
- Global reach with low-latency data centers.
- Simplified backend management.

Disadvantages:

- Requires internet connectivity.
- Higher operational costs compared to P2P.

Example: Setting up Firebase Realtime Database for AR object synchronization:

```
import firebase from "firebase/app";

import "firebase/database";

const db = firebase.database();

const objectRef = db.ref("ar_objects");

function updateARObject(objectId, position) {

objectRef.child(objectId).set(position);
```

```
}
objectRef.on("value", snapshot => {
console.log("Updated AR objects:", snapshot.val());
});
```

Real-Time Synchronization in Multi-User AR & VR

TO MAINTAIN CONSISTENCY in multi-user environments, AR & VR applications use real-time synchronization techniques:

1. State Synchronization

STATE SYNCHRONIZATION ensures that all users see the same virtual world state. This involves syncing object positions, physics interactions, and animations.

Example: Syncing player positions in a VR multiplayer game:

```
using UnityEngine;
using Photon.Pun;
public class PlayerSync : MonoBehaviourPun, IPunObservable
{
private Vector3 networkPosition;
public void OnPhotonSerializeView(PhotonStream stream, PhotonMessageInfo info)
{
if (stream.IsWriting)
```

```
{
stream.SendNext(transform.position);
}
else
{
networkPosition = (Vector3)stream.ReceiveNext();
}
}
void Update()
{
if (!photonView.IsMine)
{
transform.position = Vector3.Lerp(transform.position, networkPosition, Time.deltaTime * 5);
}
}
}
```

2. Event-Based Synchronization

INSTEAD OF CONTINUOUSLY syncing states, event-based synchronization transmits only significant changes, reducing bandwidth consumption.

Example: Broadcasting an AR event using WebSockets:

```
const socket = new WebSocket("wss://ar-server.com");

function sendEvent(eventType, data) {

socket.send(JSON.stringify({ type: eventType, data }));

}

socket.onmessage = event => {

console.log("Received AR event:", JSON.parse(event.data));

};
```

Multi-User Interaction Models

AR & VR APPLICATIONS require various interaction models to enhance collaboration and engagement:

1. Shared AR Spaces

SHARED AR SPACES ALLOW multiple users to view and interact with the same AR objects in real-world locations.

Example: ARKit shared world anchor:

```
import ARKit

let session = ARSession()

let anchor = ARAnchor(name: "SharedObject", transform: matrix_identity_float4x4)

session.add(anchor: anchor)
```

2. Virtual Avatars and Voice Chat

TO ENHANCE IMMERSION in VR, users are represented as avatars with real-time voice communication.

Example: Integrating spatial voice chat using Unity:

```
using UnityEngine;

using VivoxUnity;

public class VoiceChat : MonoBehaviour

{

private VivoxVoiceManager voiceManager;

void Start()

{

voiceManager = GetComponent<VivoxVoiceManager>();

voiceManager.Login("User1");

voiceManager.JoinChannel("VRRoom", ChannelType.Positional);

}

}
```

3. Gesture-Based Interactions

AI-POWERED GESTURE recognition enables natural interactions between users.

Example: Using OpenCV for hand gesture detection:

```
import cv2

import mediapipe as mp

mp_hands = mp.solutions.hands

hands = mp_hands.Hands()

cap = cv2.VideoCapture(0)

while cap.isOpened():

ret, frame = cap.read()

frame_rgb = cv2.cvtColor(frame, cv2.COLOR_BGR2RGB)

results = hands.process(frame_rgb)

if results.multi_hand_landmarks:

for hand_landmarks in results.multi_hand_landmarks:

print("Gesture detected")

cv2.imshow("Hand Gesture Recognition", frame)

if cv2.waitKey(1) & 0xFF == ord('q'):

break

cap.release()

cv2.destroyAllWindows()
```

Challenges in Multi-User AR & VR Development

1. **Latency and Lag** – High latency disrupts real-time interactions.
2. **Network Bandwidth Constraints** – Large AR/VR data

packets can overwhelm networks.

3. **Security and Privacy Concerns** – Protecting user data in multi-user environments is critical.
4. **Scalability Issues** – Managing thousands of concurrent users requires robust infrastructure.

Conclusion

NETWORKING IS THE BACKBONE of multi-user AR & VR experiences. By leveraging P2P, client-server, and cloud-based architectures, developers can create scalable and low-latency applications. Advanced real-time synchronization techniques, AI-driven interactions, and cloud technologies will continue to drive the evolution of shared AR & VR environments. As networking technology advances, future AR & VR experiences will become more seamless, social, and immersive.

Advanced Rendering Techniques for Realism

RENDERING IN AUGMENTED Reality (AR) and Virtual Reality (VR) plays a crucial role in delivering immersive and believable experiences. Advanced rendering techniques allow developers to create realistic lighting, shadows, reflections, and textures that enhance visual fidelity. This section explores cutting-edge rendering methods used in AR & VR, including ray tracing, global illumination, real-time reflections, advanced shader programming, and performance optimization strategies.

Importance of Advanced Rendering in AR & VR

REALISM IN AR & VR depends on accurate rendering of:

1. **Lighting and Shadows** – Realistic illumination enhances depth perception and believability.

2. **Reflections and Refractions** – Essential for creating lifelike water, glass, and metal surfaces.
3. **High-Resolution Textures** – Improves detail without excessive performance costs.
4. **Physics-Based Rendering (PBR)** – Simulates real-world material interactions.
5. **Optimized Performance** – Ensures smooth frame rates and reduces motion sickness.

Advanced rendering techniques bridge the gap between reality and digital experiences, making AR & VR environments more engaging.

Ray Tracing in AR & VR

RAY TRACING is a rendering technique that simulates the way light interacts with surfaces to produce highly realistic images. Traditionally, ray tracing has been computationally expensive, but advancements in hardware (e.g., NVIDIA RTX, AMD Radeon Ray Tracing) and software (e.g., DirectX Raytracing, Vulkan RT) enable real-time ray tracing in AR & VR.

Benefits of Ray Tracing in AR & VR

- **Physically accurate lighting** – Simulates how light bounces off surfaces.
- **Real-time reflections** – Enhances water, metal, and mirror effects.
- **Dynamic global illumination** – Improves scene realism by simulating indirect light.

Implementing Ray Tracing in Unity (C#)

```
USING UNITYENGINE;

using UnityEngine.Rendering;

public class RayTracingExample : MonoBehaviour

{

public ComputeShader rayTracingShader;

private RenderTexture target;

void Start()

{

target = new RenderTexture(Screen.width, Screen.height, 0, RenderTextureFormat.ARGBFloat);

target.enableRandomWrite = true;

target.Create();

}

void OnRenderImage(RenderTexture source, RenderTexture destination)

{

rayTracingShader.SetTexture(0, "Result", target);

rayTracingShader.Dispatch(0, Screen.width / 8, Screen.height / 8, 1);

Graphics.Blit(target, destination);
```

```
}
}
```

This script enables real-time ray tracing in Unity using compute shaders.

Global Illumination for Realistic Lighting

GLOBAL ILLUMINATION (GI) simulates how light interacts with objects in a scene, improving realism by accounting for indirect lighting.

Types of Global Illumination

1. **Precomputed GI (Baked Lighting)** – Used for static environments, reducing computational costs.
2. **Real-Time GI** – Adjusts dynamically for moving light sources and objects.
3. **Voxel-Based GI** – Utilizes voxels (3D pixels) to store lighting information for dynamic environments.

Implementing Real-Time GI in Unreal Engine (Blueprints)

1. Enable **Lumen** in Unreal Engine 5 for real-time global illumination.
2. Go to **Project Settings** → **Rendering** → Enable **Lumen Global Illumination.**
3. Adjust **Post Process Volume** → **Global Illumination Method** to **Lumen.**

Real-Time Reflections and Refractions

REFLECTIONS AND REFRACTIONS contribute significantly to realism in AR & VR by accurately simulating interactions with light.

Reflection Techniques

1. **Screen Space Reflections (SSR)** – Uses screen-space data for real-time reflections.
2. **Planar Reflections** – Computes accurate reflections on flat surfaces (e.g., mirrors).
3. **Ray-Traced Reflections** – Uses ray tracing for physically accurate reflections.

Implementing SSR in Unity (Shader Code)

```
SHADER "CUSTOM/SSRSHADER"

{

Properties

{

_Reflectivity ("Reflectivity", Range(0,1)) = 0.5

}

SubShader

{

Tags { "RenderType"="Opaque" }

Pass
```

```
{
CGPROGRAM
#pragma vertex vert
#pragma fragment frag
sampler2D _CameraDepthTexture;
float _Reflectivity;
fixed4 frag(v2f i) : SV_Target
{
float depth = tex2D(_CameraDepthTexture, i.uv).r;
return fixed4(depth * _Reflectivity, depth * _Reflectivity, depth * _Reflectivity, 1);
}
ENDCG
}
}
}
```

This shader simulates reflections using screen-space depth calculations.

Advanced Shader Programming for Realism

SHADERS PLAY A CRITICAL role in AR & VR rendering, handling everything from lighting to material properties.

Types of Shaders Used in AR & VR

1. **Vertex Shaders** – Manipulate object vertices for effects like wave animations.
2. **Fragment Shaders** – Control pixel colors for realistic materials.
3. **Compute Shaders** – Handle complex calculations like AI-driven procedural textures.

Physically Based Rendering (PBR) Shaders

PBR ENSURES THAT MATERIALS interact with light realistically by using parameters like:

- **Albedo** – Base color of the material.
- **Metallic** – Defines how much light reflects.
- **Roughness** – Controls surface smoothness.
- **Normal Maps** – Simulates surface details without additional geometry.

Example of a PBR Shader in Unity

```
SHADER "CUSTOM/PBRSHADER"
{
Properties
{
_Metallic ("Metallic", Range(0,1)) = 0.5
```

```
_Roughness ("Roughness", Range(0,1)) = 0.5
}
SubShader
{
Tags { "RenderType"="Opaque" }
Pass
{
CGPROGRAM
#pragma surface surf Standard fullforwardshadows
struct Input
{
float2 uv_MainTex;
};
void surf(Input IN, inout SurfaceOutputStandard o)
{
o.Metallic = _Metallic;
o.Smoothness = 1 - _Roughness;
}
ENDCG
}
```

```
}
}
```

Performance Optimization for AR & VR Rendering

RENDERING REALISTIC AR & VR environments requires balancing visual quality and performance. Optimization techniques include:

1. **Level of Detail (LOD)** – Reduce polygon count for distant objects.
2. **Occlusion Culling** – Render only visible objects to improve performance.
3. **Asynchronous Timewarp (ATW)** – Reduces VR motion sickness by predicting head movements.
4. **Foveated Rendering** – Renders high detail only where the user is looking.
5. **GPU Instancing** – Reduces draw calls by reusing object meshes efficiently.

Implementing Occlusion Culling in Unity

```
USING UNITYENGINE;
public class OcclusionCulling : MonoBehaviour
{
public Camera mainCamera;
public GameObject[] objects;
void Update()
{
```

```
foreach (GameObject obj in objects)

{

obj.SetActive(IsVisible(obj));

}

}

bool IsVisible(GameObject obj)

{

Plane[] planes = GeometryUtility.CalculateFrustumPlanes(mainCamera);

return GeometryUtility.TestPlanesAABB(planes, obj.GetComponent<Renderer>().bounds);

}

}
```

Future Trends in AR & VR Rendering

1. **AI-Powered Rendering** – Machine learning models improve rendering efficiency.
2. **Neural Radiance Fields (NeRFs)** – AI-generated 3D scene reconstruction.
3. **Quantum Computing for Rendering** – Quantum algorithms may revolutionize real-time rendering.
4. **Photorealistic AR Filters** – AI-enhanced AR for real-world interaction.

Conclusion

ADVANCED RENDERING techniques significantly enhance AR & VR realism by improving lighting, reflections, and material properties. Leveraging ray tracing, global illumination, advanced shaders, and performance optimizations ensures immersive and responsive experiences. As rendering technologies evolve, AR & VR will continue to push the boundaries of visual fidelity, making digital worlds indistinguishable from reality.

Chapter 7: AR & VR for Gaming and Entertainment

Game Engines for AR & VR: Unity vs. Unreal Engine

AUGMENTED REALITY (AR) and Virtual Reality (VR) game development requires powerful and versatile game engines that support immersive experiences. Among the various engines available, **Unity** and **Unreal Engine** are the two most popular choices for developers. Both offer robust tools, rendering capabilities, and cross-platform support, but they differ in usability, flexibility, and performance. This section provides an in-depth comparison of Unity and Unreal Engine for AR and VR development, their respective advantages, and practical considerations for game developers.

Choosing the Right Game Engine

SELECTING THE RIGHT game engine for an AR or VR project depends on several factors, including programming language preferences, rendering needs, performance constraints, and target platforms. Below is an overview of how Unity and Unreal Engine compare:

Feature	Unity	Unreal Engine
Programming Language	C# and JavaScript (deprecated)	C++ and Blueprints (visual scripting)
Ease of Use	Beginner-friendly, large community	Steeper learning curve, more complex
Rendering Quality	Good, customizable	Photorealistic, superior visual fidelity
Performance	Optimized for mobile and standalone VR	High-performance but resource-intensive
AR/VR Support	Supports ARKit, ARCore, Vuforia, OpenXR	Supports OpenXR, ARKit, ARCore, Oculus
Licensing	Free for small projects, paid tiers	Free until revenue exceeds $1M, then 5% royalty

Unity for AR & VR Game Development

UNITY IS ONE OF THE most widely used game engines for AR and VR due to its **ease of use, flexibility, and strong support for multiple platforms**. Many developers prefer Unity because it allows them to quickly prototype and build interactive experiences without requiring deep knowledge of graphics programming.

Advantages of Unity

- **Cross-platform Support**: Unity supports deployment to **ARKit, ARCore, OpenXR, SteamVR, Oculus, Microsoft HoloLens, and more**.

- **Asset Store**: A rich marketplace with ready-to-use assets, plugins, and tools.

- **C# Scripting**: Uses C#, which is easier for many developers compared to C++.

- **Lightweight Engine**: Performs well on mobile devices, making it a strong choice for AR.

- **Large Developer Community**: Plenty of documentation, tutorials, and support.

Setting Up an AR or VR Project in Unity

TO START A VR PROJECT in Unity using OpenXR:

1. **Install Unity Hub** and choose a version with **XR Plugin Management** support.
2. **Enable OpenXR** in **Project Settings > XR Plugin Management**.
3. **Install VR SDKs** such as **Oculus Integration** or **SteamVR Plugin** from the Unity Asset Store.
4. **Write a simple script** to implement basic VR interactions.

Here's an example script for grabbing objects in Unity using **XR Interaction Toolkit**:

```
using UnityEngine;

using UnityEngine.XR.Interaction.Toolkit;

public class GrabObject : MonoBehaviour

{

private XRGrabInteractable grabInteractable;

void Start()
```

```
{
grabInteractable = GetComponent<XRGrabInteractable>();
}
public void OnGrab()
{
Debug.Log("Object Grabbed: " + gameObject.name);
}
}
```

To use this, attach it to an object with **XRGrabInteractable** component and set up an **XR Controller**.

Unreal Engine for AR & VR Game Development

UNREAL ENGINE, DEVELOPED by **Epic Games**, is known for **high-end graphics and powerful real-time rendering**. It is the preferred choice for developers aiming for photorealistic VR experiences, especially in **PC and console VR games**.

Advantages of Unreal Engine

- **Superior Graphics**: Uses **Lumen and Nanite** for **real-time global illumination** and **high-detail models**.
- **Blueprint Visual Scripting**: Ideal for non-programmers to create interactive AR/VR experiences.

- **Optimized for VR**: Native support for **OpenXR, Oculus, and HTC Vive** with **low-latency rendering.**

- **Full Source Code Access**: Developers can modify the engine for custom needs.

Creating a VR Experience in Unreal Engine

TO BUILD A BASIC VR environment in Unreal Engine:

1. **Download and install Unreal Engine** from Epic Games Launcher.
2. **Create a new VR template project.**
3. **Enable OpenXR** in **Project Settings.**
4. **Use Blueprints** to implement teleportation and object interactions.

Example Blueprint logic for **teleportation in VR:**

- Create a **NavMesh** in the scene.

- Use the **VR Pawn** component.

- Add an **Input Action for Teleport.**

- Connect it to **Trace for Teleport Location** and **Move Player.**

Performance Optimization in AR & VR Game Engines

DEVELOPING AR AND VR games requires careful performance optimization to prevent **motion sickness, lag, and poor framerates.** Here are some key optimization techniques:

1. Reducing Draw Calls

- **Unity**: Use **static batching** and **GPU instancing**.

- **Unreal Engine**: Enable **Instanced Stereo Rendering** to optimize rendering for VR.

2. Optimizing 3D Models

- Use **low-poly models** and **Level of Detail (LOD)** for assets.

- Reduce **texture sizes** and use **compressed formats**.

3. Frame Rate Optimization

- Aim for **90+ FPS** in VR to reduce **motion sickness**.

- Use **Fixed Foveated Rendering** to prioritize center-of-view performance.

4. Memory Management

- Limit the number of **real-time shadows**.

- Reduce the **poly count** for non-essential objects.

AR & VR Development Case Studies

Case Study 1: Pokémon GO (AR)

- Developed in **Unity**.

- Uses **ARCore & ARKit** for object placement and tracking.
- Optimized for **mobile devices** with **low-power rendering.**

Case Study 2: Half-Life: Alyx (VR)

- Developed in **Source Engine** but comparable to Unreal Engine's quality.
- Uses **6DOF movement** and **interactive physics.**
- Implements **detailed hand interactions** with VR controllers.

Conclusion

BOTH UNITY AND UNREAL Engine are excellent choices for AR and VR game development. **Unity is ideal for mobile AR and lightweight VR applications**, while **Unreal Engine excels in high-fidelity, immersive VR games**. Developers should select an engine based on their **technical expertise, performance needs, and target platforms**.

By leveraging the strengths of each engine, AR and VR game developers can create **engaging, optimized, and immersive experiences** that push the boundaries of interactive entertainment.

Storytelling and Narrative Design in VR

VIRTUAL REALITY (VR) offers a unique medium for storytelling, where players are not just passive observers but active participants within the narrative. Unlike traditional forms of storytelling such as books or films, VR storytelling requires deep consideration of **presence, interactivity, and immersion** to create compelling experiences.

This section explores the **principles of narrative design in VR**, the **techniques used to engage users**, the **challenges of immersive storytelling**, and **practical strategies for implementation.**

The Fundamentals of Storytelling in VR

STORYTELLING IN VR differs significantly from traditional linear narratives. The fundamental elements include:

1. **Immersion**: The player should feel like they are inside the story rather than just observing it.
2. **Agency**: Players should have the ability to influence the story through their actions.
3. **Perspective**: First-person or third-person storytelling impacts how users engage with the narrative.
4. **Environmental Storytelling**: Instead of explicit exposition, the environment itself should communicate aspects of the story.
5. **Pacing and Flow**: The player's control over movement can affect how and when the story unfolds.

Unlike books and films, where time progresses in a linear fashion, **VR allows users to explore the narrative at their own pace**, making **non-linear storytelling** a crucial technique in VR design.

Immersive Narrative Techniques in VR

CREATING AN ENGAGING VR story requires leveraging **interactive and immersive storytelling techniques.** Below are some key techniques used in VR narrative design:

1. Diegetic Storytelling

DIEGETIC STORYTELLING means that **all narrative elements exist naturally within the world** rather than through external UI or text.

- **Example:** In **Half-Life: Alyx**, instead of displaying objectives as floating text, instructions are provided through radios or written on whiteboards within the environment.

To implement diegetic storytelling in a VR game:

- **Use audio logs**, graffiti, or computer terminals to deliver background story elements.
- **Ensure objects in the world have storytelling significance** (e.g., a broken helmet near a battlefield might indicate a past struggle).

2. Environmental Storytelling

THE ENVIRONMENT ITSELF tells a story without the need for cutscenes or dialogue. Players uncover the story by **exploring and interacting with objects**.

- **Example:** Games like **Lone Echo** and **The Walking Dead: Saints & Sinners** use environmental cues like scattered journals, graffiti, and abandoned areas to build a rich backstory.
- **Implementation in Unity:** A simple script to display a hidden message when a player interacts with an object:

```
using UnityEngine;

public class StoryElement : MonoBehaviour

{

public string message = "This object tells a story...";

void OnTriggerEnter(Collider other)

{

if (other.CompareTag("Player"))

{

Debug.Log(message);

}

}

}
```

This script can be attached to an in-game object (e.g., a book or note) to reveal a narrative hint when approached.

3. Branching Narratives and Player Choice

VR EXCELS AT **interactive storytelling**, where the user's choices influence the story. Branching narratives allow players to shape the world through decisions.

- **Example:** In **The Invisible Hours**, players can freely move through a mansion and observe different characters' perspectives, allowing for unique story progression.

- **Implementation Strategies:**
  - **Multiple endings** based on player actions.
  - **Dynamic dialogue trees** where conversations adapt to choices.
  - **Scripted events that change** based on prior interactions.

A simple branching dialogue system in Unity:

```
using UnityEngine;

public class DialogueSystem : MonoBehaviour

{

public void PlayerChoice(int choice)

{

switch (choice)

{

case 1:

Debug.Log("You chose to help the stranger.");

break;

case 2:

Debug.Log("You ignored the stranger.");

break;

}
```

```
}
}
```

Developers can expand this to include **multiple paths, consequences, and emotional weight.**

4. First-Person vs. Third-Person Perspective

THE PERSPECTIVE USED in a VR story influences **how the player experiences the narrative.**

- **First-person VR**: The player embodies the protagonist, feeling a direct connection to the story.
  - Example: **Lone Echo** (the player interacts using their own hands).
- **Third-person VR**: The player observes the character from a distance, which can help guide the story more traditionally.
  - Example: **Moss** (players control a small character while observing the world from above).

Developers should **decide early whether the player is a character in the story** or an observer shaping the narrative.

5. Non-Linear and Open-World Narratives

VR STORYTELLING OFTEN benefits from **open-world, non-linear design**, where players uncover parts of the story in a **non-sequential** manner.

- **Example:** In **The Gallery: Call of the Starseed**, players explore locations at their own pace, piecing together clues from different areas.

Developers must ensure **storytelling elements remain coherent regardless of the order in which they are discovered.**

Challenges in VR Narrative Design

1. Balancing Player Freedom with Narrative Structure

UNLIKE TRADITIONAL media, where the story unfolds at a set pace, VR allows users to **wander, ignore story cues, or interact with objects in unintended ways**. Developers must:

- **Use soft guidance mechanisms** (like lighting or sounds) to direct the player.

- **Avoid excessive cutscenes**, as they can feel restrictive in VR.

- **Ensure key story beats trigger naturally**, even if the player deviates from the intended path.

2. Motion Sickness and Pacing

FAST CAMERA MOVEMENTS, forced locomotion, or **jarring scene transitions** can cause discomfort in VR. To prevent motion sickness:

- Avoid **cutting to different angles** rapidly.

- Use **smooth locomotion options** or teleportation-based movement.

- Ensure **animations and interactions feel natural**.

3. Interactive Storytelling Without Breaking Immersion

DIALOGUE CHOICES, OBJECT interactions, and environment-based storytelling must **feel seamless** rather than like separate gameplay mechanics. Strategies include:

- **Subtle prompts** rather than intrusive UI elements.
- **Characters that acknowledge the player's presence** (e.g., NPCs reacting naturally to the player's gaze or movement).
- **Real-time physics interactions** (e.g., picking up a book should feel natural, not pre-scripted).

Best Practices for VR Narrative Design

TO CREATE **engaging VR stories**, developers should follow these best practices:

1. **Create believable worlds**: Use realistic physics, sound design, and environmental storytelling.
2. **Limit distractions**: Minimize unnecessary HUD elements and UI clutter.
3. **Encourage exploration**: Reward players for **curiosity-driven interactions**.
4. **Use immersive audio**: Spatialized audio helps guide players and enhances narrative depth.
5. **Allow meaningful choices**: Players should feel their actions impact the world.

Conclusion

STORYTELLING IN VR is a **powerful tool for immersive experiences**, combining **player agency, environmental storytelling, and interactive elements** to craft compelling narratives. By **leveraging VR's strengths**, developers can create stories that engage users in ways that traditional media cannot.

With careful design, balancing player freedom with structured storytelling, and optimizing for comfort, VR narratives can **transport players into deeply immersive worlds**, making them an integral part of the story rather than just spectators.

Creating Multiplayer and Social VR Experiences

VIRTUAL REALITY (VR) is not just a solitary experience—it thrives in multiplayer and social settings where users can **interact, collaborate, and communicate** with others in immersive environments. Multiplayer VR experiences allow users to **engage in shared worlds, compete in games, and even build virtual communities**. This section explores the fundamentals of **multiplayer VR development**, the **technical challenges involved**, and **best practices** for creating social VR interactions.

The Core Elements of Multiplayer VR

MULTIPLAYER VR IS BUILT on several key components:

1. **Networking**: The ability to **synchronize player states, actions, and environments** across different devices.
2. **Player Representation**: Avatars, gestures, and facial expressions to convey presence.
3. **Voice and Text Communication**: Spatialized audio and

chat interfaces for interaction.

4. **Social Spaces**: Shared environments where users can explore, collaborate, and play.
5. **Latency Optimization**: Minimizing lag to create a seamless multiplayer experience.
6. **Cross-Platform Compatibility**: Supporting multiple VR headsets and standalone devices.

Networking for Multiplayer VR

NETWORKING IN VR REQUIRES real-time communication between **multiple clients and a server** to keep player states synchronized. There are several networking solutions for VR development:

- **Photon PUN (Unity)**: A popular real-time multiplayer networking solution.

- **Mirror (Unity)**: A high-performance networking library for Unity-based VR games.

- **Unreal Engine Multiplayer Framework**: Built-in support for **client-server and peer-to-peer** multiplayer.

- **WebRTC & WebSockets**: Used for browser-based VR experiences (e.g., WebXR).

Basic Multiplayer Setup in Unity with Photon PUN

PHOTON PUN (PHOTON Unity Networking) is a widely used **multiplayer framework** for Unity VR applications. Below is a basic setup for **synchronizing player movements** in a multiplayer VR game.

1. Install Photon PUN in Unity:

- Open **Unity Package Manager** and import **Photon PUN 2.**
- Register on **Photon Cloud** and obtain an **App ID**.

2. Connect to a Multiplayer Room:

```
using Photon.Pun;

using UnityEngine;

public class MultiplayerManager : MonoBehaviourPunCallbacks

{

void Start()

{

PhotonNetwork.ConnectUsingSettings();

}

public override void OnConnectedToMaster()

{

PhotonNetwork.JoinLobby();

}

public override void OnJoinedLobby()

{

PhotonNetwork.JoinOrCreateRoom("VRRoom", new
Photon.Realtime.RoomOptions { MaxPlayers = 10 }, null);
```

```
}
}
```

3. Synchronizing Player Position in VR:

```
using Photon.Pun;
using UnityEngine;
public class VRPlayer : MonoBehaviourPun, IPunObservable
{
private Vector3 networkPosition;
private Quaternion networkRotation;
void Update()
{
if (photonView.IsMine)
{
// Local VR Headset tracking
transform.position = Camera.main.transform.position;
transform.rotation = Camera.main.transform.rotation;
}
else
{
// Smoothly update networked players
```

```
transform.position = Vector3.Lerp(transform.position, networkPosition, Time.deltaTime * 10);

transform.rotation = Quaternion.Lerp(transform.rotation, networkRotation, Time.deltaTime * 10);

}

}

public void OnPhotonSerializeView(PhotonStream stream, PhotonMessageInfo info)

{

if (stream.IsWriting)

{

stream.SendNext(transform.position);

stream.SendNext(transform.rotation);

}

else

{

networkPosition = (Vector3)stream.ReceiveNext();

networkRotation = (Quaternion)stream.ReceiveNext();

}

}

}
```

This simple **network synchronization** ensures that every player's position and orientation update **across all connected devices.**

Avatars and Social Interaction in VR

A CORE PART OF **social VR** is how users **see and interact with each other**. Instead of just floating controllers, players need **avatars** to represent themselves.

1. Full-body Avatars vs. Floating Hands

- **Floating Hands (Low Complexity)**: Used in games like **VRChat and Rec Room** to focus on hand interactions.
- **Full-Body Avatars (High Complexity)**: Requires **Inverse Kinematics (IK)** to estimate body movement.

2. Inverse Kinematics (IK) for Avatars

INVERSE KINEMATICS (IK) is used to **approximate full-body movement** based on head and hand positions. Unity offers **Final IK** and **VR IK** solutions.

Example IK setup:

```
using UnityEngine;

public class VRInverseKinematics : MonoBehaviour

{

public Transform head;

public Transform leftHand;
```

```
public Transform rightHand;

void Update()

{

transform.position = head.position - new Vector3(0, 1.5f, 0); // Adjust height

transform.rotation = head.rotation;

}

}
```

This script positions the player's avatar based on **head tracking**.

Voice Chat and Spatialized Audio

MULTIPLAYER VR THRIVES on **realistic communication**, and spatial audio enhances immersion. Most multiplayer VR games use:

- **Photon Voice**: Real-time voice chat for Unity VR apps.
- **Vivox**: A high-quality spatial audio SDK.
- **WebRTC Audio**: Used in WebXR-based social platforms.

Implementing Voice Chat in Photon Voice

```
USING PHOTON.VOICE.Unity;

using UnityEngine;

public class VoiceChatManager : MonoBehaviour

{
```

```
public Recorder voiceRecorder;
public Speaker voiceSpeaker;
void Start()
{
voiceRecorder.TransmitEnabled = true;
}
}
```

Designing Social VR Spaces

SOCIAL VR ENVIRONMENTS allow users to gather, chat, and engage in activities. Key considerations include:

1. **Open vs. Private Spaces**: Large public hubs vs. invite-only rooms.
2. **Object Interaction**: Users should be able to grab, throw, and manipulate objects.
3. **Emotes and Gestures**: Predefined animations and hand-tracking enhance expression.
4. **Persistence**: User-generated content should **persist across sessions** (e.g., saved avatars, drawn objects).

Reducing Latency in Multiplayer VR

LATENCY SIGNIFICANTLY impacts **multiplayer VR** by making interactions feel sluggish. To reduce latency:

1. **Use Client Prediction**: Predict user movement based on velocity.
2. **Lag Compensation**: Rewind time to match the server's last

known state.

3. **Reduce Network Traffic**: Only sync essential data (e.g., position and rotation, but not micro-movements).

Cross-Platform Multiplayer VR

MODERN VR GAMES NEED **cross-platform support** to connect users across different devices, including:

- **Standalone VR (Oculus Quest 2, Pico 4)**
- **PC VR (Valve Index, HTC Vive)**
- **WebVR (Mozilla Hubs, AltspaceVR)**

Cross-platform networking is best achieved using **Photon Fusion, WebRTC, or dedicated game servers.**

Case Study: VRChat

VRCHAT is one of the most successful **social VR** platforms. Key features include:

- **User-generated worlds and avatars**
- **Full-body tracking support**
- **Real-time multiplayer networking**
- **Built-in voice chat and emotes**

Developers can create custom VRChat worlds using **Unity and Udon scripting.**

Best Practices for Multiplayer VR Development

TO ENSURE A **seamless social VR experience**, developers should:

1. **Prioritize low-latency networking**: High response time enhances real-time interaction.
2. **Use natural interaction methods**: Gestures, head nodding, and emotes should feel intuitive.
3. **Ensure cross-platform compatibility**: Support various VR headsets and input methods.
4. **Optimize avatars for performance**: Reduce polygon count and avoid unnecessary animations.
5. **Encourage community-driven content**: User-generated worlds and avatars increase engagement.

Conclusion

MULTIPLAYER AND SOCIAL VR experiences **enhance immersion, engagement, and community building**. By implementing **real-time networking, spatialized audio, expressive avatars, and optimized latency**, developers can create compelling multiplayer VR applications that connect users in new and meaningful ways.

Monetization Strategies for AR & VR Games

AS AUGMENTED REALITY (AR) and Virtual Reality (VR) continue to grow in popularity, developers must implement effective **monetization strategies** to sustain development and generate revenue. Unlike traditional gaming, AR and VR present unique challenges and opportunities for monetization, as immersive experiences require different approaches to engagement, retention, and transactions.

This section explores the most effective **monetization models, best practices for user retention**, and **technical implementation strategies** for AR and VR game developers.

Choosing the Right Monetization Model

SELECTING THE APPROPRIATE monetization strategy depends on **game type, target audience, and platform limitations.** The most common AR and VR game monetization models include:

Monetization Model	Description
Premium Model	Players pay a one-time upfront cost to purchase the game.
Free-to-Play (F2P)	The game is free, but revenue is generated through in-app purchases or ads.
Subscription Model	Users pay a recurring fee to access the game or exclusive content.
In-App Purchases (IAP)	Players buy virtual goods, cosmetics, or other premium content.
Advertising	Monetization via in-game ads, including immersive 3D ads in VR.
Sponsorships & Brand Partnerships	Collaboration with brands to integrate sponsored content.
NFTs & Blockchain-based Models	Players buy, sell, or trade digital assets with real-world value.

Each model has its advantages and challenges. A successful strategy often involves **a combination of multiple models** to maximize revenue potential.

Premium Model: One-Time Purchase

THE **premium model** is one of the simplest monetization strategies, where players pay **a one-time upfront fee** to access the game. This model is commonly used for **high-quality, single-player VR games**.

Advantages

- Players receive a complete experience without intrusive ads.
- Works well for high-budget, story-driven VR games.
- Provides **predictable revenue per sale**.

Challenges

- High upfront cost can limit the number of potential players.
- No recurring revenue after the initial purchase.
- Requires **strong marketing efforts** to justify the price.

Example Games

- **Half-Life: Alyx (VR)**
- **Superhot VR**
- **The Walking Dead: Saints & Sinners**

Free-to-Play (F2P) Model

IN **Free-to-Play (F2P)** games, players can download and play the game for free, but revenue is generated through **in-game purchases, ads, or premium content.**

Advantages

- Lower barrier to entry results in a **larger player base.**
- Players can spend money over time instead of an upfront purchase.
- Encourages long-term engagement.

Challenges

- Requires careful balance to **avoid "pay-to-win" mechanics.**
- Monetization should feel **natural and not disrupt gameplay.**
- **Higher development and maintenance costs** for ongoing content updates.

Example Games

- **Rec Room**
- **VRChat** (monetizes through premium subscriptions and cosmetics)
- **Pokémon GO (AR)**

Implementing In-App Purchases (IAP)

IN-APP PURCHASES (IAP) allow players to buy **virtual goods, cosmetics, upgrades, or premium content**. This model is widely used in AR and VR games to drive long-term revenue.

Types of IAP in AR & VR

1. **Cosmetics** – Skins, avatars, or clothing (e.g., **VRChat Avatars**).
2. **Virtual Currency** – Players purchase coins or gems for in-game transactions.
3. **Gameplay Enhancements** – Boosts, extra levels, or weapons.
4. **Unlockable Content** – Expansion packs, new characters, or storylines.

Implementing IAP in Unity (VR Example)

TO ENABLE IN-APP PURCHASES in Unity, developers can use the **Unity IAP package**:

```
using UnityEngine;

using UnityEngine.Purchasing;

public class IAPManager : MonoBehaviour

{

public void BuyItem(string itemID)

{

CodelessIAPStoreListener.Instance.InitiatePurchase(itemID);
```

```
}
}
```

Players can purchase items within the VR interface by linking the **itemID** to a virtual store.

Subscription-Based Monetization

A **subscription model** provides users with access to content on a **monthly or yearly basis.** This model is popular for **social VR platforms and continuous content updates.**

Advantages

- Generates **recurring revenue.**
- Encourages **user retention** and long-term engagement.
- Works well for **live-service** and **multiplayer experiences.**

Challenges

- Requires **constant content updates** to justify recurring payments.
- Users may **cancel subscriptions if they don't see ongoing value.**

Example Games & Platforms

- **Rec Room Plus** – Provides exclusive content and in-game currency.

- **Oculus Quest+ Subscription** – Monthly access to select VR games.

- **Supernatural (VR Fitness App)** – Subscription-based fitness workouts.

Advertising in AR & VR Games

ADS IN TRADITIONAL mobile games are straightforward, but in AR and VR, **advertising must be immersive and non-intrusive.** Instead of static banners, developers use **native ads that integrate with the VR world.**

Types of VR Advertising

1. **3D In-World Ads** – Billboards or posters inside VR environments.
2. **Sponsored Items** – Branded clothing, weapons, or cosmetics.
3. **Rewarded Ads** – Players watch an ad to earn in-game rewards.
4. **Product Placement** – Real-world brands integrated into the virtual world.

Example Implementation of VR Ads

USING **Unity Ads** in VR, developers can reward players for watching ads:

```
using UnityEngine;

using UnityEngine.Advertisements;

public class VRAdManager : MonoBehaviour
```

```
{
public void ShowRewardedAd()
{
if (Advertisement.IsReady("rewardedVideo"))
{
Advertisement.Show("rewardedVideo");
}
}
}
```

Players watch ads in **exchange for in-game rewards**, keeping them engaged while generating revenue.

Sponsorships and Brand Partnerships

MANY AR AND VR GAMES **partner with brands** to create exclusive, branded content. This method is highly effective in **sports, entertainment, and fitness applications**.

Examples of Successful Partnerships

- **Nike in Fortnite (Virtual Sneaker Skins)**
- **Star Wars in Beat Saber (DLC Song Packs)**
- **Pokémon GO's Sponsored Locations (McDonald's, Starbucks, etc.)**

NFTs and Blockchain-Based Monetization

BLOCKCHAIN AND NFTS (Non-Fungible Tokens) provide a way for players to **own and trade virtual assets with real-world value.** While still controversial, some VR and AR platforms are experimenting with NFTs.

Use Cases

- **Virtual Land Sales** – Players buy digital real estate in games like **Decentraland.**
- **NFT Avatars & Skins** – Unique, tradeable skins for avatars.
- **Blockchain-Based Economies** – Players earn cryptocurrency by participating in virtual experiences.

Best Practices for AR & VR Monetization

TO ENSURE A **successful and sustainable** monetization strategy in AR and VR games, developers should follow these best practices:

1. **Prioritize User Experience** – Avoid intrusive monetization that breaks immersion.
2. **Offer Value Through Purchases** – Ensure that IAPs provide meaningful benefits.
3. **Balance Free and Paid Content** – Free-to-play games should not feel overly "pay-to-win."
4. **Encourage Community Engagement** – Social elements like avatar customization drive spending.
5. **Regularly Update Content** – Subscription models require frequent new content to retain users.
6. **Optimize Performance** – Poorly integrated ads or

transactions can degrade the user experience.

Conclusion

MONETIZING AR AND VR games requires a **careful balance between profitability and player experience**. The best strategies combine **free-to-play models, subscriptions, IAPs, and immersive advertising** while ensuring **players feel engaged and rewarded**. By implementing smart monetization techniques, developers can create **sustainable, profitable AR & VR experiences** while keeping users immersed in their virtual worlds.

Chapter 8: AR & VR in Business and Enterprise Solutions

AR & VR for Training and Education

Introduction

AUGMENTED REALITY (AR) and Virtual Reality (VR) are revolutionizing the way businesses and institutions approach training and education. These immersive technologies offer experiential learning opportunities that are more effective, engaging, and interactive than traditional training methods. From corporate training programs to medical simulations and educational curricula, AR and VR are transforming knowledge transfer and skill development across various industries.

This section explores the applications, benefits, implementation strategies, and real-world case studies of AR and VR in training and education.

Benefits of AR & VR in Training and Education

AR AND VR PROVIDE SEVERAL advantages over conventional training approaches:

1. **Immersive Learning** – VR creates fully immersive environments where users can practice real-world scenarios safely, while AR overlays interactive information on real-world settings.
2. **Increased Engagement** – The interactive nature of AR and VR enhances engagement and retention compared to passive learning.
3. **Safe and Risk-Free Training** – Dangerous or high-risk

tasks can be practiced virtually, minimizing real-world risks.

4. **Cost-Effective** – Reduces the need for physical training materials, travel, and instructor-led training sessions.
5. **Personalized Learning Paths** – AI-driven VR and AR experiences can adapt to the learner's pace and preferences.
6. **Real-Time Feedback and Assessment** – Trainers can track progress, analyze performance data, and provide instant feedback.
7. **Remote Learning Opportunities** – AR and VR enable remote training sessions, reducing geographical limitations.

Applications of AR & VR in Training and Education

1. Corporate Training and Professional Development

MANY CORPORATIONS ARE leveraging AR and VR to train employees in various domains:

- **Onboarding Programs** – VR tours help new hires familiarize themselves with the workplace and processes before they physically start work.

- **Soft Skills Training** – Virtual reality simulations allow employees to practice public speaking, conflict resolution, leadership, and negotiation.

- **Technical and Safety Training** – Industries such as manufacturing, oil and gas, and aviation use VR simulations to train employees on machinery operation, safety protocols, and emergency response procedures.

Example: A manufacturing company uses VR to train employees on machine operation without requiring access to physical equipment. This reduces downtime and prevents accidents.

2. Medical and Healthcare Training

AR AND VR PLAY A CRUCIAL role in medical education by providing hands-on experience in a controlled environment:

- **Surgical Simulations** – VR-based simulations allow medical students and surgeons to practice complex procedures without real patients.

- **Anatomy Education** – AR applications overlay 3D models of the human body, enabling students to explore anatomy interactively.

- **Patient Care Training** – VR scenarios help nurses and doctors develop bedside manner, empathy, and diagnostic skills.

Example: A medical school implements VR surgical simulations, enabling students to practice procedures repeatedly before performing them on real patients.

3. K-12 and Higher Education

AR AND VR ARE TRANSFORMING traditional classroom learning by making it interactive and experiential:

- **History and Geography** – VR enables students to visit historical sites and geographical locations virtually.

- **STEM Learning** – AR applications bring abstract science and math concepts to life with interactive 3D models.

- **Language Learning** – VR immersion in foreign language environments enhances conversational skills and comprehension.

Example: A history teacher uses VR to transport students to ancient Rome, allowing them to explore the city as it existed centuries ago.

4. Military and Defense Training

THE MILITARY USES AR and VR for combat training, vehicle operation, and battlefield simulations:

- **Flight Simulators** – VR-based flight training helps pilots practice takeoff, navigation, and emergency maneuvers.

- **Combat Readiness** – Soldiers undergo tactical training in realistic VR environments, preparing them for real-world combat.

- **Mission Planning** – AR-enhanced maps provide real-time situational awareness for soldiers and commanders.

Example: A defense organization develops VR combat training programs that replicate real-world battlefield conditions, improving soldiers' decision-making skills.

5. Vocational and Skilled Trades Training

AR AND VR ASSIST IN skill-based training for construction, automotive repair, and other trades:

- **Electrician Training** – AR overlays show wiring diagrams and step-by-step guidance for electrical installations.

- **Automotive Repair** – VR simulations allow mechanics to practice diagnostics and repairs on virtual engines.

- **Construction and Architecture** – VR enables architects to visualize building designs before construction begins.

Example: An automotive school integrates AR-guided repair instructions, allowing students to interact with 3D engine models while learning about components.

Implementing AR & VR Training Programs

TO SUCCESSFULLY INTEGRATE AR and VR into training and education, organizations should follow these key steps:

1. **Identify Learning Objectives**

   ○ Define what skills or knowledge the training aims to impart.

   ○ Determine whether AR, VR, or a combination is most suitable.

2. **Choose the Right Hardware and Software**

○ Select AR headsets (e.g., Microsoft HoloLens, Magic Leap) or VR headsets (e.g., Oculus Quest, HTC Vive, PlayStation VR).

○ Use appropriate platforms such as Unity, Unreal Engine, or WebXR.

3. **Develop Engaging and Interactive Content**

○ Create 3D models, animations, and realistic simulations.

○ Integrate AI and gamification elements for an adaptive learning experience.

4. **Pilot and Test the Training Module**

○ Conduct a trial phase with a small group of learners.

○ Gather feedback and refine the experience based on user insights.

5. **Deploy at Scale and Monitor Performance**

○ Implement across the organization or institution.

○ Track engagement, effectiveness, and user progress using analytics tools.

Sample Code: Creating an AR Learning Experience with Unity and ARKit

HERE'S A BASIC EXAMPLE of how to create an AR educational app using Unity and ARKit:

```
using UnityEngine;
```

```
using UnityEngine.XR.ARFoundation;

using UnityEngine.XR.ARSubsystems;

public class ARLearningExperience : MonoBehaviour

{

private ARRaycastManager arRaycastManager;

private List<ARRaycastHit> hits = new List<ARRaycastHit>();

public GameObject educationalObject; // Assign a 3D model of an
educational content

void Start()

{

arRaycastManager = GetComponent<ARRaycastManager>();

}

void Update()

{

if (Input.touchCount > 0)

{

Touch touch = Input.GetTouch(0);

if (arRaycastManager.Raycast(touch.position, hits,
TrackableType.PlaneWithinPolygon))

{

Pose hitPose = hits[0].pose;
```

```
Instantiate(educationalObject, hitPose.position, hitPose.rotation);
}
}
}
}
```

Case Study: Walmart's VR Employee Training

WALMART HAS IMPLEMENTED VR-based training across its stores using the Oculus platform. The training modules simulate real-world customer service scenarios, emergency procedures, and sales floor management. By using VR, Walmart has reported improved employee confidence and retention rates.

Future Trends in AR & VR Training

THE FUTURE OF AR AND VR in training and education will be shaped by advancements in AI, cloud computing, and 5G technology. Key trends include:

- **AI-Powered Adaptive Learning** – AI will personalize VR training based on user performance.
- **Multi-User VR Classrooms** – Virtual classrooms will allow real-time collaboration and interaction.
- **Haptic Feedback and Wearables** – Advanced haptic gloves and suits will enhance realism in VR training.
- **Augmented Workspaces** – AR will integrate seamlessly into work environments for real-time assistance.

Conclusion

AR AND VR ARE TRANSFORMING training and education by making learning immersive, interactive, and effective. From corporate onboarding to medical simulations, these technologies are reshaping how knowledge is delivered and retained. As hardware and software continue to evolve, AR and VR will become indispensable tools in education and professional development.

AR & VR in Healthcare and Therapy

Introduction

AUGMENTED REALITY (AR) and Virtual Reality (VR) have emerged as transformative technologies in the healthcare industry, reshaping patient care, medical training, diagnostics, and therapeutic applications. These immersive tools offer real-time visualizations, interactive simulations, and personalized treatment solutions, improving the efficiency and effectiveness of medical interventions.

The integration of AR and VR in healthcare spans across multiple domains, including surgical planning, pain management, physical rehabilitation, mental health therapy, and patient education. This section explores their applications, benefits, challenges, and future prospects.

Benefits of AR & VR in Healthcare

1. **Enhanced Medical Training** – AR and VR provide interactive, hands-on experiences for medical students and professionals, allowing them to practice procedures in a risk-free environment.
2. **Improved Patient Outcomes** – These technologies help doctors make more accurate diagnoses and perform precise

surgeries through real-time augmented visuals.

3. **Non-Invasive Treatment Options** – VR-based therapy is being used for pain management, mental health treatment, and rehabilitation.
4. **Remote Healthcare Services** – AR-enabled telemedicine enhances remote consultations, providing doctors with real-time insights into a patient's condition.
5. **Reduced Costs and Risks** – Simulated medical procedures reduce the need for expensive medical equipment and lower the risk of surgical errors.

Applications of AR & VR in Healthcare

1. Medical Training and Surgical Simulation

TRADITIONAL MEDICAL training relies on textbooks, lectures, and limited hands-on practice. AR and VR address these limitations by offering:

- **Anatomy Visualization:** AR applications overlay 3D models of human anatomy onto physical spaces, allowing students to explore organs, muscles, and the circulatory system interactively.

- **Surgical Training:** VR enables surgeons to practice complex procedures in a virtual operating room, reducing reliance on cadavers and real-life trials.

- **Remote Learning:** AR and VR allow medical trainees to attend interactive virtual lectures and participate in collaborative surgeries.

Example: Harvard Medical School has integrated VR-based anatomy lessons into its curriculum, allowing students to manipulate 3D models of human organs in a virtual environment.

2. Augmented Surgery and Preoperative Planning

AR AND VR ENHANCE SURGICAL precision by providing real-time visual overlays and 3D imaging:

- **AR-Assisted Surgery:** Surgeons use AR headsets, such as Microsoft HoloLens, to overlay MRI and CT scan images onto a patient's body during surgery.
- **3D Preoperative Planning:** VR simulations enable doctors to rehearse surgeries before performing them on actual patients.
- **Minimally Invasive Procedures:** AR provides real-time guidance during endoscopic and laparoscopic surgeries.

Example: Johns Hopkins Hospital successfully performed an AR-guided spinal surgery, allowing surgeons to visualize internal structures with enhanced accuracy.

3. Pain Management and Physical Rehabilitation

VR-BASED THERAPY IS revolutionizing pain management and rehabilitation by providing distraction-based treatments and interactive exercises:

- **Pain Reduction:** VR experiences help burn victims and post-operative patients reduce pain by immersing them in calming virtual environments.

- **Stroke Rehabilitation:** VR-based physical therapy guides stroke survivors through rehabilitative exercises, improving mobility and motor function.

- **Phantom Limb Pain Treatment:** VR allows amputees to visualize and interact with a virtual limb, helping them manage phantom limb pain.

Example: The SnowWorld VR application has been used to help burn patients manage pain by immersing them in a snowy virtual landscape while undergoing treatment.

4. Mental Health Therapy and Cognitive Rehabilitation

AR AND VR ARE WIDELY used in mental health treatments, including:

- **Exposure Therapy:** VR exposes patients to controlled environments to help them overcome phobias, PTSD, and anxiety.

- **Cognitive Behavioral Therapy (CBT):** VR-based CBT allows therapists to create immersive scenarios for patients dealing with depression, OCD, and PTSD.

- **Mindfulness and Stress Reduction:** VR meditation apps transport users to serene virtual landscapes to help reduce stress and anxiety.

Example: The VR therapy platform "Bravemind" is used by the U.S. Department of Veterans Affairs to treat PTSD in military personnel by exposing them to virtual combat scenarios in a controlled setting.

5. AR-Enabled Telemedicine and Remote Diagnostics

WITH THE RISE OF TELEHEALTH, AR is enhancing remote consultations by:

- **AR-Based Remote Examinations:** Doctors can use AR overlays to examine patients virtually, guiding them through self-examinations with real-time feedback.

- **Smart Glasses for Diagnoses:** Physicians can wear AR glasses to access patient records and real-time diagnostic data during telemedicine calls.

- **AI-Powered Symptom Analysis:** AI-driven AR applications analyze symptoms and provide preliminary diagnoses before a patient visits a doctor.

Example: The Vuzix Blade AR glasses allow doctors to perform remote consultations with real-time medical data overlays, improving diagnostic accuracy.

Implementing AR & VR in Healthcare

1. Choosing the Right Hardware

DIFFERENT AR AND VR devices are used based on the medical application:

- **AR Headsets:** Microsoft HoloLens, Magic Leap, and Google Glass are commonly used for augmented surgeries and remote consultations.

- **VR Headsets:** Oculus Rift, HTC Vive, and PlayStation VR are used for training, therapy, and rehabilitation.

- **Haptic Gloves and Feedback Devices:** These enhance tactile feedback for surgical simulations and physical therapy.

2. Selecting Development Platforms and Software

HEALTHCARE APPLICATIONS are built using advanced AR and VR development platforms:

- **Unity and Unreal Engine:** Used for creating VR simulations and medical training applications.

- **ARKit and ARCore:** Apple's and Google's frameworks for developing AR healthcare apps.

- **Custom Medical Software:** Platforms like Touch Surgery and Osso VR provide specialized medical training tools.

3. Regulatory Compliance and Data Security

SINCE HEALTHCARE APPLICATIONS handle sensitive patient data, compliance with regulations such as HIPAA (Health Insurance Portability and Accountability Act) and GDPR (General Data Protection Regulation) is critical. Developers must ensure:

- **Secure Data Encryption:** Protecting patient information from breaches.

- **Anonymization of Patient Data:** Ensuring patient privacy.

- **Ethical Use of AR & VR:** Avoiding bias and misinformation in medical simulations.

Sample Code: VR-Based Medical Training in Unity

THE FOLLOWING UNITY C# script demonstrates a simple VR training module for medical students to interact with a 3D anatomical model:

```
using UnityEngine;

using UnityEngine.XR.Interaction.Toolkit;

public class VRMedicalTraining : MonoBehaviour

{

public XRGrabInteractable organModel; // Assign a 3D organ model in Unity

void Start()

{

organModel.onSelectEntered.AddListener(ShowOrganDetails);

}

void ShowOrganDetails(XRBaseInteractor interactor)

{
```

```
Debug.Log("Organ Selected: " + organModel.name);
// Display detailed information about the organ
}
}
```

Future Trends in AR & VR Healthcare Applications

THE FUTURE OF AR AND VR in healthcare is driven by technological advancements in AI, machine learning, and 5G connectivity. Key trends include:

- **AI-Enhanced Diagnostics:** AI-powered AR applications will assist doctors in identifying diseases based on real-time patient data.
- **Haptic Feedback for Surgery:** Advanced haptic gloves will allow surgeons to "feel" virtual tissues during remote procedures.
- **AR for Remote Surgeries:** 5G-enabled AR will facilitate telesurgery, allowing experts to guide procedures from anywhere in the world.
- **Neuro-VR Therapy:** VR simulations will be used to treat neurodegenerative disorders such as Alzheimer's and Parkinson's.

Conclusion

AR AND VR ARE RESHAPING the healthcare industry by providing innovative solutions for medical training, surgery, pain management, mental health treatment, and telemedicine. As these technologies continue to advance, they will become integral to modern medicine, improving patient outcomes, reducing healthcare costs, and enhancing medical education. The adoption of AR and VR in healthcare is expected to accelerate, paving the way for a future where immersive technology plays a crucial role in saving lives and improving global healthcare accessibility.

Retail, Real Estate, and E-Commerce Applications

Introduction

AUGMENTED REALITY (AR) and Virtual Reality (VR) are transforming the retail, real estate, and e-commerce industries by enhancing customer experiences, streamlining business operations, and providing immersive engagement opportunities. These technologies bridge the gap between digital and physical shopping, allowing consumers to visualize products in real-world contexts, experience virtual property tours, and make informed purchasing decisions without stepping out of their homes.

In real estate, AR and VR provide interactive property showcases, allowing potential buyers and renters to explore properties remotely. In retail and e-commerce, these technologies enable virtual try-ons, product visualization, and immersive shopping experiences that boost customer confidence and sales. This section explores the applications, benefits, challenges, and future prospects of AR and VR in these industries.

Benefits of AR & VR in Retail, Real Estate, and E-Commerce

1. **Enhanced Customer Engagement** – Interactive AR and

VR experiences keep customers engaged, increasing brand loyalty and conversion rates.

2. **Improved Decision-Making** – Virtual try-ons, product visualizations, and 3D store walkthroughs help customers make better purchasing decisions.
3. **Remote Accessibility** – Virtual real estate tours and immersive online shopping allow global customers to explore properties and products remotely.
4. **Personalized Shopping Experiences** – AI-powered AR and VR applications customize product recommendations based on user preferences.
5. **Reduced Returns and Costs** – AR-based product previews minimize buyer uncertainty, reducing return rates in e-commerce.
6. **Competitive Differentiation** – Companies leveraging AR and VR gain a technological edge over competitors.

Applications of AR & VR in Retail

1. Virtual Try-Ons and Smart Mirrors

AR-POWERED VIRTUAL try-ons allow customers to visualize clothing, accessories, and makeup in real-time using their smartphone or AR mirrors in stores.

- **Fashion and Apparel** – Brands like Gucci and Nike enable customers to see how shoes, clothes, and accessories look on them through AR apps.

- **Cosmetics and Beauty** – Companies like L'Oréal and Sephora offer AR-powered makeup try-ons.

- **Eyewear and Jewelry** – Virtual try-on tools allow customers to see how glasses and jewelry look on their faces.

Example:

Sephora's Virtual Artist app uses AR to let users try on different makeup products before purchasing.

2. Augmented Shopping Assistants

RETAILERS ARE USING AR-based shopping assistants to guide customers through stores, offering product information and personalized recommendations.

- **In-Store Navigation** – AR-powered wayfinding apps help customers locate products in large stores.

- **Product Information Overlays** – AR apps scan barcodes to display detailed product information, including reviews and price comparisons.

Example:

IKEA Place allows users to place AR furniture in their homes before buying, ensuring size and style compatibility.

3. Immersive VR Shopping Experiences

VIRTUAL REALITY IS redefining online shopping by providing fully immersive store environments.

- **Virtual Stores** – Brands like Tommy Hilfiger and Alibaba have launched VR stores where customers can walk through a virtual showroom.

- **Live VR Shopping Events** – Companies host live VR shopping events, allowing customers to interact with products and brand representatives in real-time.

Example:

Walmart's VR shopping experience enables users to explore a virtual store and purchase products without leaving home.

Applications of AR & VR in Real Estate

1. Virtual Property Tours

VR-BASED PROPERTY TOURS allow buyers and renters to explore homes, apartments, and commercial spaces remotely.

- **360° VR Walkthroughs** – Prospective buyers can navigate properties in full VR, eliminating the need for physical visits.

- **Remote Real Estate Viewings** – International buyers can tour properties remotely before making a purchase decision.

- **Historical and Future Visualization** – AR overlays show renovations, future developments, or historical restorations.

Example:

Zillow's 3D Home feature provides VR tours of listed properties, allowing potential buyers to explore homes virtually.

2. AR-Enhanced Interior Design and Home Staging

AR APPLICATIONS HELP buyers visualize home decor, furniture placement, and renovations before making a purchase.

- **Furniture Placement** – AR apps allow users to place virtual furniture inside a space.
- **Home Customization** – AR tools let homeowners experiment with paint colors, flooring, and decor.

Example:

Houzz's AR feature allows users to visualize how furniture and home decor will look in their space before making a purchase.

3. Smart Property Management and Maintenance

AR-BASED PROPERTY MANAGEMENT tools assist real estate professionals and tenants in maintaining properties efficiently.

- **AR Building Inspections** – Inspectors use AR headsets to overlay structural data on buildings.
- **Maintenance Assistance** – Tenants use AR apps to receive step-by-step maintenance instructions for common repairs.

Example:

Magicplan enables property managers to create AR floor plans and visualize renovations.

Applications of AR & VR in E-Commerce

1. 3D Product Visualization

E-COMMERCE PLATFORMS are integrating AR and VR to help customers view products in 3D before purchasing.

- **Virtual Showrooms** – Online retailers offer 3D product previews, allowing customers to inspect items from all angles.
- **Product Size and Fit Visualization** – AR overlays display how products will fit into real-world spaces.

Example:

Amazon's AR View lets users place virtual products in their homes before purchasing.

2. AR-Enabled Customer Support

AR-POWERED SUPPORT tools help customers troubleshoot issues without requiring in-person assistance.

- **AR Product Assembly Guides** – Interactive AR instructions assist users in assembling furniture and electronics.
- **Remote AR Support** – Customer service representatives use AR annotations to guide customers through troubleshooting steps.

Example:

Bosch's AR-based customer support provides real-time visual assistance for home appliances and tools.

Implementing AR & VR in Retail, Real Estate, and E-Commerce

1. Choosing the Right AR/VR Hardware

DIFFERENT INDUSTRIES require specific AR and VR hardware:

- **AR Devices:** Smartphones, AR headsets (HoloLens, Magic Leap), and smart glasses.
- **VR Devices:** Oculus Rift, HTC Vive, PlayStation VR, and standalone headsets.
- **Haptic Devices:** Gloves and suits that provide tactile feedback for immersive shopping and property tours.

2. Selecting Development Platforms

AR AND VR APPLICATIONS for retail, real estate, and e-commerce are built using:

- **Unity and Unreal Engine** – Used for VR shopping and real estate experiences.
- **ARKit (Apple) and ARCore (Google)** – Mobile AR applications.

- **WebXR and Three.js** – Web-based AR and VR experiences.

3. Security and Data Privacy Considerations

WITH INCREASED ADOPTION of AR and VR in commerce, ensuring customer data protection is critical:

- **Data Encryption** – Protects sensitive customer information.

- **User Anonymity** – Prevents personal data collection without consent.

- **Secure Transactions** – AR/VR payment gateways must comply with industry security standards.

Sample Code: AR Product Visualization in Unity

THE FOLLOWING UNITY C# script demonstrates an AR-based product visualization feature for an e-commerce app:

```
using UnityEngine;

using UnityEngine.XR.ARFoundation;

using UnityEngine.XR.ARSubsystems;

public class ARProductPlacement : MonoBehaviour

{

private ARRaycastManager arRaycastManager;

private List<ARRaycastHit> hits = new List<ARRaycastHit>();
```

```
public GameObject productPrefab; // Assign a 3D product model
void Start()
{
arRaycastManager = GetComponent<ARRaycastManager>();
}
void Update()
{
if (Input.touchCount > 0)
{
Touch touch = Input.GetTouch(0);
if (arRaycastManager.Raycast(touch.position, hits,
TrackableType.PlaneWithinPolygon))
{
Pose hitPose = hits[0].pose;
Instantiate(productPrefab, hitPose.position, hitPose.rotation);
}
}
}
}
```

Future Trends in AR & VR for Commerce

THE FUTURE OF AR AND VR in retail, real estate, and e-commerce will be shaped by:

- **AI-Powered AR Shopping Assistants** – AI-driven AR assistants will provide real-time shopping recommendations.
- **Metaverse Commerce** – Virtual malls and immersive shopping experiences will redefine online retail.
- **Blockchain-Powered Virtual Ownership** – NFTs and blockchain will enable secure virtual property ownership in real estate and e-commerce.

Conclusion

AR AND VR ARE REVOLUTIONIZING retail, real estate, and e-commerce by creating immersive, interactive, and personalized customer experiences. These technologies improve decision-making, reduce costs, and enhance engagement, paving the way for the future of digital commerce. As technology continues to evolve, AR and VR will play an even greater role in shaping how consumers shop, explore properties, and interact with businesses.

Future Business Opportunities in AR & VR

Introduction

THE RAPID ADVANCEMENT of Augmented Reality (AR) and Virtual Reality (VR) is unlocking new business opportunities across multiple industries. As hardware becomes more accessible and software continues to evolve, businesses are exploring innovative ways to integrate immersive technology into their operations. From next-generation remote work solutions to fully immersive digital commerce, AR and VR are shaping the future of business.

This section delves into emerging AR and .VR business opportunities, their market potential, implementation strategies, and key challenges. Companies that embrace these technologies early will gain a competitive advantage in the evolving digital economy.

Market Potential and Growth of AR & VR in Business

1. **Projected Growth** – The AR and VR market is expected to surpass $250 billion by 2030, driven by advancements in hardware, AI integration, and widespread adoption across industries.
2. **Cross-Industry Adoption** – AR and VR are transforming industries such as healthcare, retail, real estate, finance, and manufacturing.
3. **Metaverse Integration** – The rise of virtual worlds and digital economies presents new opportunities for businesses to establish immersive experiences and virtual marketplaces.
4. **5G and Cloud Computing** – High-speed internet and cloud-based processing enhance the accessibility and performance of AR and VR applications.
5. **AI and Machine Learning Synergy** – AI-driven AR and VR applications enable real-time personalization, automation, and intelligent interactions.

Emerging Business Opportunities in AR & VR

1. Immersive Remote Work and Collaboration

WITH THE SHIFT TOWARD remote and hybrid work environments, businesses are investing in AR and VR for virtual offices, training, and collaboration.

- **Virtual Offices and Meeting Spaces** – Companies use VR platforms like Spatial and Horizon Workrooms to conduct meetings in immersive digital environments.
- **Remote Team Training** – AR-based training programs provide real-time guidance, reducing the need for physical training centers.
- **3D Data Visualization** – VR dashboards help businesses analyze complex data interactively.

Example:

Microsoft's Mesh platform allows teams to meet in shared VR spaces, enhancing remote collaboration.

2. AR-Powered Smart Cities and Urban Planning

GOVERNMENTS AND ENTERPRISES are leveraging AR for urban planning, infrastructure development, and smart city management.

- **City Planning Simulations** – VR environments enable planners to visualize new developments before construction.

- **AR Navigation and Wayfinding** – Smart glasses and AR apps provide real-time navigation assistance in urban areas.

- **Infrastructure Maintenance** – AR overlays assist engineers in visualizing underground utilities and structures.

Example:

Singapore's Virtual Singapore project uses AR and VR for city planning and real-time monitoring of urban development.

3. VR-Based Tourism and Cultural Experiences

THE TRAVEL INDUSTRY is incorporating AR and VR to enhance tourism and cultural experiences.

- **Virtual Travel Experiences** – Users can explore world landmarks and historical sites without leaving their homes.

- **AR-Enhanced Museums and Exhibits** – Museums use AR to provide interactive storytelling and digital reconstructions.

- **VR Hotel Previews** – Travelers can tour hotels in VR before making bookings.

Example:

Google Earth VR allows users to experience global destinations in immersive virtual environments.

4. AR and VR in Manufacturing and Industry 4.0

AR AND VR ARE REVOLUTIONIZING manufacturing by improving design, prototyping, and training.

- **Digital Twin Technology** – AR-based digital twins allow real-time monitoring of industrial equipment.

- **VR Factory Simulations** – Manufacturers use VR to optimize factory layouts and improve operational efficiency.

- **Remote Equipment Maintenance** – AR headsets guide technicians through equipment repairs using real-time overlays.

Example:

Boeing uses AR-powered smart glasses to assist engineers in assembling aircraft components with higher precision.

5. AR in Financial Services and Fintech

THE FINANCIAL SECTOR is adopting AR to improve customer engagement, data visualization, and banking experiences.

- **AR Banking Apps** – Customers can view account details and transaction history through AR interfaces.

- **VR Stock Market Simulations** – Traders analyze market trends using VR-based 3D financial dashboards.

- **Cryptocurrency and Metaverse Banking** – VR banks and digital currencies are emerging in the metaverse.

Example:

Mastercard is exploring AR payment systems, allowing users to make transactions through smart glasses.

6. AR and VR in Personalized Marketing

BRANDS ARE USING AR and VR to create highly personalized and immersive marketing campaigns.

- **AR Advertising** – Interactive AR ads engage users through gamification and real-world interactions.
- **VR Brand Experiences** – Companies create branded VR worlds where users can explore products and services.
- **AI-Powered AR Recommendations** – Machine learning tailors AR experiences to individual user preferences.

Example:

Coca-Cola has developed AR experiences that allow customers to interact with their products through mobile apps.

Implementing AR & VR Business Strategies

1. Choosing the Right Business Model

BUSINESSES SHOULD ADOPT AR and VR models based on their industry and target audience:

• **Subscription-Based Services** – VR training platforms, virtual offices, and AR business tools operate on a subscription model.

• **E-Commerce and Digital Sales** – Brands integrate AR product previews and VR shopping experiences.

• **Advertising and Sponsorships** – Companies monetize VR content through in-game ads and sponsored virtual experiences.

2. Selecting AR & VR Development Platforms

BUSINESSES CAN LEVERAGE existing AR and VR development platforms to build applications:

• **Unity and Unreal Engine** – Used for creating immersive VR experiences and AR applications.

• **WebAR and WebXR** – Browser-based AR and VR experiences eliminate the need for dedicated apps.

• **AI Integration Platforms** – AI-enhanced AR applications provide smart recommendations and automation.

3. Addressing Key Business Challenges

WHILE AR AND VR OFFER immense opportunities, businesses must address key challenges:

• **High Development Costs** – AR and VR applications require significant investment in hardware, software, and talent.

- **User Adoption and Accessibility** – Ensuring seamless user experiences and reducing entry barriers.
- **Privacy and Security Risks** – Protecting user data and maintaining ethical AR/VR practices.

Sample Code: AR Navigation for Business Locations

THE FOLLOWING UNITY C# script demonstrates an AR wayfinding application for guiding customers through a business location:

```
using UnityEngine;

using UnityEngine.XR.ARFoundation;

using UnityEngine.XR.ARSubsystems;

public class ARNavigation : MonoBehaviour

{

private ARRaycastManager arRaycastManager;

private List<ARRaycastHit> hits = new List<ARRaycastHit>();

public GameObject waypointPrefab; // Assign a 3D waypoint model

void Start()

{

arRaycastManager = GetComponent<ARRaycastManager>();

}

void Update()
```

```
{
if (Input.touchCount > 0)
{
Touch touch = Input.GetTouch(0);
if (arRaycastManager.Raycast(touch.position, hits, TrackableType.Planes))
{
Pose hitPose = hits[0].pose;
Instantiate(waypointPrefab, hitPose.position, hitPose.rotation);
}
}
}
}
```

Future Trends in AR & VR Business Innovations

THE FUTURE OF AR AND VR in business will be driven by AI, blockchain, and cloud computing. Key trends include:

- **AI-Powered Virtual Assistants** – AI-driven avatars will provide customer service and business support in VR environments.
- **Blockchain-Enabled AR & VR Transactions** – Secure and decentralized transactions will facilitate virtual commerce.

- **Holographic Telepresence** – Businesses will use holographic AR for remote collaboration and customer interactions.

- **Neural Interface VR** – Brain-computer interfaces (BCIs) will enable direct interaction with virtual environments.

Conclusion

AR AND VR ARE OPENING new frontiers in business, transforming industries ranging from finance and manufacturing to retail and urban planning. Companies that invest in these technologies will gain a significant competitive advantage in the digital economy. As AR and VR hardware becomes more advanced and accessible, the next decade will see a surge in immersive business applications that redefine how people work, shop, and interact in virtual and augmented environments.

Chapter 9: Testing, Debugging, and Deployment

Debugging Tools and Performance Optimization

TESTING AND DEBUGGING are critical steps in AR & VR development, ensuring that applications function smoothly, maintain performance, and provide an immersive user experience. Due to the complexity of real-time rendering, motion tracking, and hardware variations, developers must adopt a systematic approach to identifying and resolving issues.

This section covers the essential debugging tools, techniques for performance optimization, and best practices for testing AR & VR applications.

Debugging AR & VR Applications

DEBUGGING AR & VR APPLICATIONS is more challenging than traditional software due to the integration of 3D graphics, sensors, and real-time interactions. Developers must use specialized debugging tools to identify rendering issues, latency problems, and hardware compatibility concerns.

Common Issues in AR & VR Debugging

1. **Rendering and Frame Rate Drops**

   ○ Symptoms: Laggy or stuttering visuals, delayed object rendering

○ Cause: High computational load, unoptimized shaders, excessive draw calls

○ Solution: Optimize assets, reduce polygon count, implement occlusion culling

2. **Tracking and Sensor Inconsistencies**

○ Symptoms: Jittery or incorrect motion tracking, inconsistent positioning

○ Cause: Poor lighting (for optical tracking), sensor drift, interference

○ Solution: Calibrate tracking hardware, use sensor fusion techniques, optimize marker detection

3. **Interaction Bugs**

○ Symptoms: Controllers not responding, hand tracking issues

○ Cause: Misconfigured input mapping, API incompatibilities

○ Solution: Ensure correct SDK usage, log input events, debug interaction logic

4. **Latency and Motion Sickness**

○ Symptoms: Nausea, dizziness, unresponsive movements

○ Cause: High motion-to-photon latency, frame rate fluctuations

○ Solution: Aim for 90 FPS in VR, implement asynchronous timewarp, optimize rendering pipeline

5. **Platform-Specific Bugs**

○ Symptoms: Application crashes on specific devices, inconsistent rendering

○ Cause: Differences in ARKit (iOS) vs. ARCore (Android) or VR SDK variations

○ Solution: Test on multiple devices, handle platform-specific optimizations

---

Debugging Tools for AR & VR Development

VARIOUS TOOLS EXIST to help developers debug and optimize AR & VR applications:

1. Unity Debugging Tools

- **Unity Profiler**: Monitors CPU, GPU, and memory usage.
- **Frame Debugger**: Step through frame rendering to analyze draw calls.
- **XR Interaction Debugging**: Examines input handling for controllers and sensors.
- **OVR Metrics Tool** (for Oculus): Monitors real-time performance on Quest devices.

2. Unreal Engine Debugging Tools

- **GPU Visualizer**: Analyzes GPU usage and bottlenecks.
- **Stat Commands** (stat unit, stat fps): Displays real-time performance metrics.
- **RenderDoc**: Captures frames for debugging rendering issues.
- **VR Template Debugging Console**: Provides real-time insights into VR interactions.

3. AR & VR Platform-Specific Tools

- **ARKit Developer Console** (iOS)
- **ARCore Debugging Tools** (Android)
- **SteamVR Performance Test**
- **OpenXR Debugging Tools**

4. General Debugging Tools

- **Visual Studio Debugger**: For step-through debugging in C# projects.
- **Chrome Developer Tools** (for WebAR/WebVR).
- **ADB (Android Debug Bridge)**: Logs Android device output for AR debugging.

Performance Optimization Techniques

OPTIMIZING PERFORMANCE is crucial for ensuring a smooth and comfortable AR & VR experience. High frame rates (at least 60 FPS for AR, 90 FPS for VR) and low latency (below 20ms motion-to-photon) are necessary for user comfort.

1. Reducing Render Load

- **Level of Detail (LOD) Optimization**: Use lower-poly models at a distance.
- **Occlusion Culling**: Do not render objects not visible to the user.
- **Baked Lighting**: Reduce real-time lighting calculations.
- **Efficient Shaders**: Avoid expensive fragment shader operations.

2. Memory Management

- **Reduce Texture Size**: Compress textures using formats like ASTC, ETC2.
- **Object Pooling**: Reuse frequently instantiated objects to reduce garbage collection.
- **Lazy Loading**: Load assets on demand rather than all at once.

3. Motion and Interaction Optimization

- **Predictive Tracking**: Use machine learning models to predict user movement.
- **Timewarp/Spacewarp**: Oculus and SteamVR techniques to interpolate frames.
- **Optimize Physics Calculations**: Reduce unnecessary physics computations in VR scenes.

4. Network Optimization for Multi-User AR/VR

- **Lag Compensation**: Implement interpolation and extrapolation for networked experiences.
- **Efficient Data Synchronization**: Send only necessary data, compress packets.
- **Edge Computing**: Offload computations closer to the user to reduce latency.

Code Example: Profiling in Unity

```
USING UNITYENGINE;

using UnityEngine.Profiling;

public class PerformanceProfiler : MonoBehaviour

{

void Update()

{
```

```
Debug.Log("Frame Time: " + Time.deltaTime);

Debug.Log("Memory Usage: " + Profiler.GetTotalAllocatedMemoryLong());

}

}
```

This script logs frame time and memory usage to help identify performance bottlenecks.

Code Example: Debugging VR Controller Input

```
USING UNITYENGINE;

using UnityEngine.XR;

public class ControllerDebugger : MonoBehaviour

{

void Update()

{

foreach (XRNodeState node in InputTracking.GetNodeStates())

{

Debug.Log("Device: " + node.nodeType + " - Position: " + node.position);

}

}

}
```

This script prints the positions of VR controllers, helping debug input issues.

Best Practices for Debugging and Performance Optimization

1. **Test on Physical Devices**

○ Emulators do not always replicate real-world AR & VR behavior.

2. **Use Logging and Breakpoints Effectively**

○ Print sensor data, frame rates, and interactions in development builds.

3. **Minimize Draw Calls**

○ Reduce the number of objects rendered per frame.

4. **Optimize Code Execution**

○ Avoid expensive computations in Update() for Unity or Tick() for Unreal.

5. **Balance Visual Quality and Performance**

○ Aim for a balance between realistic rendering and maintaining frame rates.

6. **Leverage Platform-Specific Optimizations**

○ Use ARKit's scene reconstruction or ARCore's depth API for efficiency.

7. **Optimize Asset Loading**

○ Load assets asynchronously to prevent blocking the main thread.

8. **Monitor Frame Rates and Memory Usage Regularly**

○ Set up automated profiling during development.

Conclusion

DEBUGGING AND OPTIMIZING AR & VR applications is a complex but essential part of the development process. By leveraging specialized debugging tools, addressing common performance pitfalls, and adopting best practices, developers can create immersive, responsive, and high-performance experiences.

The next section will cover **User Testing and Feedback Collection**, exploring strategies for validating AR & VR applications through real-world testing.

User Testing and Feedback Collection

USER TESTING IS A CRUCIAL step in AR & VR development, ensuring that applications are intuitive, immersive, and free from usability issues. Unlike traditional applications, AR & VR experiences rely heavily on real-time interactions, spatial awareness, and sensory feedback. This makes structured user testing even more essential for detecting comfort issues, motion sickness, and usability flaws.

This section covers best practices for user testing, different testing methodologies, tools for collecting feedback, and how to iterate based on user insights.

Importance of User Testing in AR & VR

USER TESTING IN AR & VR applications goes beyond functional testing; it focuses on **user comfort, interaction accuracy, and immersion quality**. Key reasons for conducting extensive user testing include:

1. **Detecting Motion Sickness and Discomfort**

○ VR experiences with high latency, low frame rates, or excessive movement can cause nausea.

○ AR applications with jittery tracking or awkward controls may frustrate users.

○ Testing helps fine-tune motion dynamics and adjust rendering settings for comfort.

2. **Ensuring Intuitive Interactions**

○ Unlike mobile or desktop applications, AR & VR use unique inputs (hand tracking, voice commands, controllers).

○ Poorly designed interactions lead to frustration and reduced usability.

○ Testing reveals usability flaws and helps refine user interfaces.

3. **Evaluating Spatial Awareness and Object Placement**

○ AR applications rely on accurate spatial mapping and object placement in the real world.

○ VR experiences require realistic depth perception and occlusion handling.

○ Testing helps detect inconsistencies and fine-tune placement algorithms.

4. **Enhancing Performance Across Devices**

○ AR & VR applications run on a variety of devices with different hardware capabilities.

○ Performance can vary significantly based on CPU, GPU, and tracking sensors.

○ Testing across multiple devices ensures smooth performance for all users.

5. **Gathering Real-World Feedback**

○ Developers may overlook usability flaws due to familiarity with their own application.

○ End users provide fresh perspectives on usability, immersion, and overall experience.

○ Feedback helps prioritize feature improvements and bug fixes.

Types of AR & VR User Testing

DIFFERENT TYPES OF testing methodologies help identify various issues in AR & VR applications. Some of the most effective user testing approaches include:

1. Exploratory Testing

- Involves observing users interact with the application naturally.
- Helps identify unexpected usability challenges.
- Ideal for early-stage prototypes.

2. Usability Testing

- Focuses on how easily users can perform specific tasks.
- Measures efficiency, ease of navigation, and interaction design quality.
- Can be conducted with structured tasks or open-ended exploration.

3. A/B Testing

- Compares two versions of an interface or interaction method.
- Helps determine which approach works better for user experience.
- Useful for refining UI layouts, control schemes, and comfort settings.

4. Performance Testing

- Measures frame rates, latency, and rendering speed.

- Identifies bottlenecks in motion tracking and interaction processing.
- Ensures the application runs smoothly across different devices.

5. Motion Sickness Testing

- Conducted to assess how the application affects users prone to VR sickness.
- Users rate their comfort levels during various interactions.
- Helps optimize motion settings like snap turning and teleportation.

6. Accessibility Testing

- Focuses on making AR & VR applications inclusive for all users.
- Tests for usability by individuals with disabilities or limitations.
- Involves alternative input methods (voice commands, eye tracking, etc.).

Planning a User Testing Session

A STRUCTURED APPROACH to user testing ensures reliable and actionable feedback. The following steps outline how to plan and conduct an effective AR & VR user testing session:

Step 1: Define Testing Goals

BEFORE CONDUCTING USER testing, developers should identify:

- Specific features or interactions to test.
- Performance benchmarks (frame rate, latency, tracking accuracy).
- Comfort and usability metrics.

Step 2: Select Test Participants

CHOOSING THE RIGHT test users is crucial:

- Include both experienced AR/VR users and newcomers.
- Consider users with different levels of motion sickness sensitivity.
- Test on a variety of hardware configurations.

Step 3: Set Up the Testing Environment

- Ensure a safe space for VR movement (clear obstacles).
- Prepare devices and headsets with tracking systems calibrated.
- Minimize external factors (lighting conditions for AR, background noise).

Step 4: Define Testing Scenarios

- Give users specific tasks to complete, such as:
    - Navigating a VR environment.
    - Interacting with AR objects.
    - Performing gestures or using controllers.
- Observe how users naturally attempt these tasks.

Step 5: Record User Interactions

- Use screen recordings, eye-tracking data, and motion logs.
- Note where users struggle or experience discomfort.
- Collect real-time feedback through verbal comments.

Step 6: Conduct Post-Test Interviews

- Ask users about their experience:
    - What was easy or difficult?
    - Did they feel motion sickness?
    - Were controls intuitive?
- Encourage honest, detailed feedback.

Step 7: Analyze Data and Iterate

- Identify common issues reported by multiple users.

- Prioritize critical fixes (motion sickness, usability barriers).

- Implement improvements and conduct additional testing if necessary.

Tools for Collecting Feedback

VARIOUS TOOLS HELP streamline user feedback collection in AR & VR testing:

1. **Observation & Screen Recording**

○ **OBS Studio**: Records VR gameplay and user interactions.

○ **Unity Recorder**: Captures in-game AR/VR footage for analysis.

2. **Analytics & Heatmaps**

○ **Google Firebase Analytics**: Tracks user interactions in AR apps.

○ **Oculus Developer Tools**: Provides usage and performance data.

○ **Cognitive3D**: Generates heatmaps for user focus areas in VR.

3. **Eye-Tracking Analysis**

○ **Tobii Eye Tracker**: Analyzes where users look in VR experiences.

○ **Pupil Labs**: Offers detailed gaze-tracking for AR applications.

4. **User Feedback Collection**

○ **Google Forms**: Simple surveys for structured feedback.

○ **Typeform**: Interactive forms with open-ended responses.

○ **Qualtrics**: Advanced user research and analytics.

Code Example: Implementing a User Feedback Form in Unity

THIS SCRIPT COLLECTS user feedback after an AR/VR session and sends it to a database.

```
using UnityEngine;

using UnityEngine.UI;

using System.Collections;

using System.Net.Http;

public class FeedbackForm : MonoBehaviour

{

public InputField feedbackInput;

public Button submitButton;

void Start()

{
```

```
submitButton.onClick.AddListener(SendFeedback);
}
void SendFeedback()
{
string feedback = feedbackInput.text;
StartCoroutine(SendFeedbackToServer(feedback));
}
IEnumerator SendFeedbackToServer(string feedback)
{
string url = "https://yourserver.com/api/feedback";
WWWForm form = new WWWForm();
form.AddField("feedback", feedback);
using (UnityWebRequest www = UnityWebRequest.Post(url, form))
{
yield return www.SendWebRequest();
if (www.result == UnityWebRequest.Result.Success)
Debug.Log("Feedback sent successfully!");
else
Debug.LogError("Error sending feedback: " + www.error);
}
```

```
}
}
```

This script creates a basic UI form where users can submit feedback, which is then uploaded to a server.

Best Practices for Iterating Based on User Feedback

- **Prioritize Critical Fixes First**: Address major comfort and usability issues before cosmetic changes.
- **Test Updates with Users**: Ensure that fixes actually improve the experience.
- **Document All Findings**: Maintain records of user complaints and resolutions.
- **Refine UI & Controls**: Make adjustments based on common interaction difficulties.
- **Optimize Performance Continuously**: Keep refining frame rates, latency, and motion responsiveness.

Conclusion

USER TESTING AND FEEDBACK collection are essential for refining AR & VR applications, ensuring usability, comfort, and engagement. By structuring testing sessions effectively, utilizing the right tools, and iterating based on feedback, developers can create immersive experiences that resonate with users.

The next section will explore **Deploying AR & VR Applications to Various Platforms**, covering distribution methods, platform-specific requirements, and best practices for release management.

Deploying AR & VR Applications to Various Platforms

DEPLOYING AN AR OR VR application involves packaging, distributing, and optimizing the application for different platforms, ensuring compatibility across devices, and following platform-specific guidelines. Unlike traditional mobile or desktop apps, AR & VR applications require additional considerations such as hardware compatibility, rendering performance, and platform-specific SDKs.

This section covers best practices for deploying AR & VR applications, platform-specific requirements, distribution methods, and post-deployment maintenance.

Understanding Deployment Requirements for AR & VR Platforms

BEFORE DEPLOYING AN AR or VR application, it is crucial to understand the requirements of different platforms. Each platform has its own SDKs, store policies, and performance expectations.

Platform	Primary SDKs	Supported Devices	Distribution Channels
Oculus (Meta Quest, Rift, Go)	Oculus SDK, OpenXR	Quest 2, Quest 3, Rift S, Go	Oculus Store, SideQuest
SteamVR	OpenVR, OpenXR	HTC Vive, Valve Index, Oculus	Steam Store
PlayStation VR	PSVR SDK	PS4, PS5 with PSVR headset	PlayStation Store
ARKit (iOS)	ARKit	iPhones, iPads	Apple App Store
ARCore (Android)	ARCore	Android smartphones	Google Play Store
Microsoft HoloLens	Mixed Reality Toolkit (MRTK), OpenXR	HoloLens 2, Windows MR headsets	Microsoft Store
WebAR & WebVR	Three.js, WebXR API	Browsers (Chrome, Firefox, Edge)	Hosted Web Apps

Each platform has specific submission requirements, and failing to meet these can result in rejection from official stores.

Preparing an AR & VR Application for Deployment

1. Optimize for Performance

BEFORE SUBMITTING AN AR or VR application, performance optimization is critical to ensure smooth rendering and responsiveness.

- **Frame Rate Targeting:** Aim for 60 FPS (AR), 90+ FPS (VR) to avoid motion sickness.
- **Occlusion Culling:** Only render objects visible to the user.
- **Texture and Model Optimization:** Use compressed textures and reduce polycount.
- **LOD (Level of Detail) Scaling:** Load lower-resolution models at a distance.
- **Memory Management:** Optimize garbage collection and object pooling.

2. Implement Cross-Platform Compatibility

IF TARGETING MULTIPLE platforms, consider using **OpenXR** for VR applications and **AR Foundation** for AR applications.

```
using UnityEngine;

using UnityEngine.XR.ARFoundation;

public class PlatformDetection : MonoBehaviour

{

void Start()

{

if (Application.platform == RuntimePlatform.Android)

Debug.Log("Running on Android with ARCore");

else if (Application.platform == RuntimePlatform.IPhonePlayer)
```

```
Debug.Log("Running on iOS with ARKit");
}
}
```

This script detects the platform and ensures compatibility.

3. Build and Package the Application

EACH PLATFORM HAS DIFFERENT build requirements:

- **Oculus Quest:** Export as an **Android APK** with Oculus XR Plugin.
- **SteamVR:** Export as a **Windows executable** with OpenVR SDK.
- **PlayStation VR:** Requires a **Sony Developer Account** and PSVR SDK.
- **ARKit (iOS):** Must be compiled with Xcode and signed with an Apple Developer ID.
- **ARCore (Android):** Export as an APK with ARCore dependencies.
- **HoloLens:** Package as a UWP (Universal Windows Platform) app.

Submitting to App Stores

1. Oculus Store Submission (Meta Quest, Rift)

- Register as an Oculus Developer.
- Create an **Oculus App ID** in the Oculus Developer Dashboard.
- Package the application using **Oculus Developer Hub (ODH)**.
- Submit for review with the required assets:
  - Game trailer
  - Screenshots
  - Description & metadata
- Pass **Oculus' VRC (Virtual Reality Checks)** to ensure performance and comfort.

2. SteamVR Submission (HTC Vive, Valve Index)

- Register as a **Steamworks Developer**.
- Upload the game build via **SteamPipe**.
- Configure **App Manifest** with supported controllers and headsets.
- Submit for SteamVR performance testing.

3. PlayStation VR Submission

- Apply for **Sony's PlayStation Developer Program**.
- Use the **PSVR SDK** and ensure compatibility.
- Pass Sony's **QA process**, including:
  - Comfort testing
  - Controller compatibility
  - Store UI integration

4. Apple App Store Submission (ARKit Apps)

- Enroll in the **Apple Developer Program**.
- Use **Xcode** to sign and submit the app.
- Enable **ARKit Capabilities** in the Info.plist file.

```
<KEY>NSCAMERAUSAGEDESCRIPTION</key>

<string>This app requires camera access for Augmented Reality.</string>

<key>ARKit</key>

<true/>
```

5. Google Play Store Submission (ARCore Apps)

- Register as a **Google Play Developer**.
- Package the APK and test using **Google Play Console**.

- Ensure **AR Required Flag** is set in the AndroidManifest.xml:

```
<META-DATA ANDROID:NAME="com.google.ar.core"
android:value="required" />
```

Alternative Distribution Methods

IF THE APP IS NOT BEING submitted to official stores, alternative distribution methods include:

1. **SideQuest (For Oculus Quest)**

○ Allows sideloading VR applications without going through the official Oculus Store.

○ Useful for beta testing before an official launch.

2. **APK Direct Download (For Android AR)**

○ Applications can be distributed via a direct APK download from a website.

○ Requires users to enable "Install from Unknown Sources."

3. **WebAR & WebVR Hosting**

○ Web-based AR & VR applications can be hosted on platforms like **Glitch, GitHub Pages, or AWS S3**.

○ Example of embedding a WebXR scene:

```
<a-scene webxr>

<a-box position="0 1 -3" color="blue"></a-box>
```

```
</a-scene>
```

Post-Deployment Maintenance

AFTER DEPLOYMENT, REGULAR updates and maintenance are necessary to keep the application stable and up-to-date.

1. Collect User Feedback

- Monitor store reviews and user complaints.
- Use crash reporting tools like **Firebase Crashlytics** for AR apps.
- Enable telemetry tracking for VR performance data.

2. Update for SDK Changes

- ARKit and ARCore receive frequent updates, which may require changes to app functionality.
- Oculus and SteamVR SDKs also update tracking algorithms and input handling.

3. Monitor Performance and Compatibility

- As new devices launch, compatibility testing should continue.
- Optimize for new hardware (e.g., next-generation VR headsets).

4. **Security & Privacy Considerations**

- Ensure data collected from AR applications (camera, location) complies with **GDPR** and **CCPA** regulations.
- VR multiplayer applications must follow **user safety guidelines** to prevent harassment.

Best Practices for a Successful Deployment

1. **Test Across Multiple Devices**

○ Ensure the app works on different screen sizes, VR controllers, and tracking systems.

2. **Optimize Load Times**

○ AR & VR applications should minimize startup time to improve user retention.

3. **Enable Beta Testing Before Public Release**

○ Use **TestFlight** (iOS), **Google Play Beta**, or **Oculus App Lab** for pre-release testing.

4. **Prepare for Store Review Delays**

○ Apple and PlayStation can take up to 2 weeks for approval.

○ Plan updates accordingly to avoid unnecessary downtime.

5. **Monitor Updates to Platform Policies**

○ Stores like Oculus and Steam frequently update their submission guidelines.

Conclusion

DEPLOYING AN AR & VR application involves careful consideration of platform requirements, performance optimization, and distribution strategies. By following best practices for packaging, submission, and post-deployment maintenance, developers can ensure a smooth launch and a successful user experience.

The next section will focus on **Maintaining and Updating AR & VR Projects**, discussing long-term support strategies, bug fixes, and evolving with new technology trends.

Maintaining and Updating AR & VR Projects

MAINTAINING AND UPDATING an AR or VR application is essential for ensuring continued functionality, compatibility with evolving hardware and software, and an optimal user experience. Unlike traditional applications, AR & VR projects require frequent updates due to advancements in tracking algorithms, device firmware updates, and changing platform requirements.

This section explores best practices for long-term maintenance, versioning strategies, update deployment, bug fixing, and handling user feedback for ongoing improvements.

Importance of Maintenance in AR & VR Projects

MAINTAINING AN AR OR VR application involves more than just fixing bugs. It requires a proactive approach to **performance**

optimization, feature enhancements, security updates, and ensuring compatibility with new devices.

1. Ensuring Compatibility with New Hardware

- AR & VR hardware evolves rapidly, with frequent updates to tracking technology and input methods.
- Applications must be tested on new devices to ensure they function correctly.
- Example: A VR game built for **Oculus Quest 2** might need optimizations for **Quest 3**.

2. Updating for Platform and SDK Changes

- Major AR & VR platforms (ARKit, ARCore, Oculus SDK, SteamVR) receive frequent updates.
- Failure to update may lead to deprecations, causing app instability or store removal.
- Example: **ARKit 6** introduced new depth APIs, requiring adjustments for older ARKit 5 applications.

3. Improving Performance Over Time

- Performance optimization is an ongoing process, ensuring smooth frame rates and reduced latency.
- Reducing memory usage and improving load times can significantly enhance the user experience.

- Example: Implementing **adaptive quality scaling** to maintain 90 FPS in VR.

4. Fixing Bugs and User-Reported Issues

- Post-launch, real-world usage may reveal bugs missed in testing.
- A structured **bug tracking and resolution process** is essential for maintaining quality.

5. Enhancing Features Based on User Feedback

- Continuous iteration improves user retention and satisfaction.
- AR & VR applications should evolve with user needs and emerging interaction trends.

Versioning and Update Strategies

1. Semantic Versioning for AR & VR Applications

MAJOR.MINOR.PATCH

- **Major Updates (X.0.0)** – Significant feature updates, breaking changes, or major redesigns.
- **Minor Updates (X.Y.0)** – New features that do not break existing functionality.

- **Patch Updates (X.Y.Z)** – Bug fixes and performance improvements.

Example:

- **1.0.0** – Initial launch
- **1.1.0** – Added new VR locomotion system
- **1.1.1** – Fixed minor controller tracking bug
- **2.0.0** – Overhauled UI and introduced multiplayer mode

2. Managing Backward Compatibility

- Ensure that updates do not break support for older hardware unless necessary.
- Provide **legacy support modes** for devices with lower processing power.
- Example: Allow users on **Oculus Quest 1** to disable advanced rendering features introduced for **Quest 3**.

3. Handling API Deprecations

- Platforms may phase out older APIs, requiring refactoring.
- Regularly check SDK documentation for upcoming deprecations.
- Example: **SteamVR switched from OpenVR to OpenXR**, requiring migration.

Automating Updates and Patch Deployment

UPDATING AN AR OR VR application across multiple platforms can be time-consuming. Automating deployment ensures efficiency and reduces errors.

1. Continuous Integration (CI) and Continuous Deployment (CD)

- Automate build and deployment using tools like:
  - **GitHub Actions**
  - **Jenkins**
  - **CircleCI**
- Implement automatic build testing to catch errors before release.

EXAMPLE GITHUB ACTIONS workflow for a Unity VR project:

name: Build and Deploy VR App

on:

push:

branches:

- main

jobs:

build:

```
runs-on: ubuntu-latest

steps:

- name: Checkout Code

uses: actions/checkout@v2

- name: Setup Unity

uses: game-ci/unity-builder@v2

- name: Build for Oculus Quest

run: ./build.sh—platform android—target OculusQuest

- name: Upload Build

uses: actions/upload-artifact@v2

with:

name: VR-App-Build

path: ./Builds/OculusQuest.apk
```

This workflow automatically builds and uploads a new version whenever code is pushed to the main branch.

2. Cloud-Based Patch Delivery

- Use cloud platforms like **AWS S3** or **Firebase Hosting** to deliver updates.
- Enable **incremental updates** to reduce download size.

Debugging and Fixing Bugs in Live AR & VR

Applications

ONCE AN AR OR VR APPLICATION is live, debugging becomes more challenging. Remote debugging and logging tools help identify and fix issues efficiently.

1. Remote Logging and Crash Reporting

- Implement crash logging to capture errors occurring on user devices.
- Tools:
  - **Sentry** – Real-time error tracking
  - **Firebase Crashlytics** – Monitors app stability
  - **Unity Cloud Diagnostics** – Collects AR/VR crash reports

EXAMPLE OF INTEGRATING Firebase Crashlytics in Unity:

```
using Firebase;

using Firebase.Crashlytics;

using UnityEngine;

public class CrashLogger : MonoBehaviour

{

void Start()

{
```

```
FirebaseApp.CheckAndFixDependenciesAsync().ContinueWith(task
=>

{

if (task.Result == DependencyStatus.Available)

Crashlytics.ReportUncaughtExceptionsAsFatal = true;

});

}

}
```

2. Monitoring Performance in Live Applications

- Monitor FPS, memory usage, and CPU/GPU performance.
- Use **OVR Metrics Tool** (for Oculus) or **SteamVR Performance Profiler**.

User Feedback and Community Engagement

LISTENING TO USERS helps improve the application and build a loyal community.

1. Collecting Feedback

- Use in-app surveys or external platforms (Google Forms, Typeform).
- Implement a **feedback button** in the app UI.

- Monitor store reviews and social media discussions.

2. Community Engagement

- Engage with users on Discord, Reddit, and VR/AR forums.
- Provide regular updates and respond to bug reports.
- Host **beta testing programs** for early access users.

EXAMPLE OF SENDING user feedback to a database:

```
using UnityEngine;
using UnityEngine.Networking;
using System.Collections;
public class FeedbackSender : MonoBehaviour
{
public string feedback;
void SendFeedback()
{
StartCoroutine(PostFeedback(feedback));
}
IEnumerator PostFeedback(string feedbackText)
{
WWWForm form = new WWWForm();
```

```
form.AddField("feedback", feedbackText);

using (UnityWebRequest request = UnityWebRequest.Post("https://yourserver.com/feedback", form))

{

yield return request.SendWebRequest();

if (request.result == UnityWebRequest.Result.Success)

Debug.Log("Feedback sent!");

else

Debug.LogError("Error sending feedback: " + request.error);

}

}

}
```

Security Considerations in AR & VR Maintenance

- **Data Privacy Compliance**
  - Ensure compliance with **GDPR** (Europe), **CCPA** (California), and **HIPAA** (Healthcare).
  - Avoid excessive data collection.
- **Preventing Cheating and Exploits in Multiplayer VR**
  - Use **server-side validation** for game logic.

○ Encrypt network traffic to prevent **man-in-the-middle attacks**.

- **Protecting User Identity in Social VR**

○ Implement **privacy filters** (e.g., muting/blocking tools in VR chat apps).

○ Ensure user avatars and interactions comply with safety guidelines.

Long-Term Support and Evolution of AR & VR Projects

A SUCCESSFUL AR OR VR project should evolve with technological advancements and user expectations.

1. Regular Feature Updates

- Add **new locomotion methods** (e.g., teleportation, hand tracking).
- Improve haptics and feedback mechanisms.

2. Supporting Emerging Devices

- Test on new hardware (e.g., Apple Vision Pro, Meta Quest 4).
- Implement **adaptive rendering techniques** for future-proofing.

3. Open-Source and Modding Support

- Providing **modding APIs** can extend application lifespan.
- Example: VRChat's open modding framework allows users to create custom experiences.

Conclusion

MAINTAINING AND UPDATING AR & VR applications is a continuous process that ensures compatibility, stability, and user satisfaction. By implementing structured update strategies, automated deployment, proactive bug tracking, and community engagement, developers can extend the lifespan of their projects and keep users engaged.

With maintenance in place, developers can focus on **future innovation and expanding AR & VR capabilities.**

Chapter 10: The Future of AR & VR

Trends and Innovations in AR & VR Technology

AUGMENTED REALITY (AR) and Virtual Reality (VR) technologies continue to evolve at a rapid pace, driven by advancements in hardware, software, and user experience innovations. The future of AR and VR is shaping up to be more immersive, accessible, and integrated into various aspects of our daily lives. This section explores the major trends and innovations that are shaping the future of AR & VR technology, from hardware improvements to artificial intelligence (AI) integration, cloud computing, and emerging applications.

1. Advancements in AR & VR Hardware

ONE OF THE KEY DRIVERS of AR and VR adoption is the continuous improvement in hardware, making devices more powerful, compact, and affordable. Some of the most notable advancements include:

- **Higher-Resolution Displays**: Modern VR headsets now feature ultra-high-resolution displays with higher refresh rates (120Hz or more), reducing the screen-door effect and enhancing immersion.

- **Lighter and More Ergonomic Designs**: Manufacturers are focusing on making AR/VR headsets lighter and more comfortable for extended use. This includes reducing weight, improving balance, and designing headsets with better ventilation.

- **Wireless and Standalone Headsets**: The shift from tethered to standalone headsets, such as the Meta Quest series, enables greater mobility and convenience, eliminating the need for powerful external computers.

- **Foveated Rendering and Eye-Tracking**: Advanced eye-tracking allows for foveated rendering, where only the area a user is looking at is rendered in full resolution, significantly improving performance.

- **Haptic Feedback and Motion Interfaces**: Devices such as haptic gloves, full-body tracking suits, and tactile feedback controllers enhance the sense of touch in virtual environments, making interactions more natural and immersive.

2. Artificial Intelligence (AI) in AR & VR

AI PLAYS A SIGNIFICANT role in enhancing AR and VR experiences by enabling intelligent interactions, automation, and personalization. Key AI-driven advancements include:

- **Computer Vision for AR Applications**: AI-driven computer vision allows AR devices to better understand and interact with the real world, improving object recognition, spatial mapping, and gesture recognition.

- **Natural Language Processing (NLP) for Voice Control**: AI-powered NLP enables voice interactions within VR environments, allowing users to communicate naturally with virtual assistants, NPCs, or even other users.

- **Procedural Content Generation**: AI can dynamically generate 3D environments, characters, and scenarios in real-time, enhancing the scalability of VR worlds for gaming, training, and simulation applications.

- **AI-Driven Personalization**: Machine learning algorithms analyze user behavior and preferences to tailor AR/VR experiences, offering customized recommendations and interactive environments.

3. Cloud Computing and Edge Processing

CLOUD COMPUTING AND edge computing are transforming the way AR and VR applications process and render content, reducing latency and enabling more complex experiences.

- **Cloud Rendering for VR**: Instead of requiring high-end local GPUs, cloud-based rendering services process VR graphics remotely and stream the content to the headset in real-time.

- **AR Streaming Over 5G**: With 5G networks, AR applications can stream large-scale 3D models and interactive content without requiring high-end processing power on local devices.

- **Edge AI Processing**: AI algorithms run on edge devices instead of centralized cloud servers, reducing data transmission times and improving real-time responsiveness for AR and VR applications.

4. AR & VR in the Metaverse

THE CONCEPT OF THE Metaverse—a persistent, immersive digital universe—relies heavily on advancements in AR and VR technology. The future Metaverse aims to integrate virtual workspaces, social interactions, entertainment, and commerce into a seamless experience.

- **Persistent Virtual Worlds**: VR will facilitate digital economies, social interactions, and persistent virtual spaces that users can access anytime.
- **AR Enhancing Everyday Life**: AR glasses will overlay digital information onto the real world, providing real-time data, navigation, and collaboration tools.
- **Decentralized Digital Assets**: Blockchain and NFTs are expected to play a role in virtual asset ownership, digital goods trading, and monetization of virtual spaces.

5. Next-Generation Interaction Methods

THE WAY USERS INTERACT with AR and VR environments is evolving beyond traditional controllers and keyboards. New interaction methods include:

- **Hand and Finger Tracking**: Advances in sensor technology allow for precise hand-tracking without the need for external controllers, making interactions more intuitive.
- **Brain-Computer Interfaces (BCIs)**: Emerging research in BCIs enables users to control AR and VR

experiences using brain activity, opening doors for new accessibility solutions.

- **Tactile and Force Feedback Devices**: Haptic vests, pressure-sensitive gloves, and force-feedback controllers enhance the realism of physical interactions within VR.

6. The Rise of AR Smart Glasses

AR SMART GLASSES ARE set to replace smartphones as the primary interface for digital interactions. Some key developments include:

- **Lightweight, Everyday Wearables**: Companies such as Apple, Meta, and Google are investing in AR glasses that can be worn all day without discomfort.

- **Integration with AI Assistants**: AR glasses will seamlessly integrate with AI-powered digital assistants, enabling real-time translations, contextual awareness, and smart reminders.

- **Augmented Productivity**: Future AR glasses will revolutionize workplace productivity by overlaying digital interfaces onto real-world tasks, such as virtual whiteboards and real-time collaboration tools.

7. Expansion of AR & VR in Various Industries

BEYOND GAMING AND ENTERTAINMENT, AR and VR technologies are making significant impacts in multiple industries:

- **Healthcare**: VR is being used for surgical simulations, mental health therapy, and pain management, while AR assists in real-time diagnostics and remote surgeries.

- **Education and Training**: AR and VR provide immersive learning environments for students, allowing for hands-on experience in fields such as medicine, engineering, and aviation.

- **Retail and E-Commerce**: Virtual showrooms, AR-powered try-ons, and immersive shopping experiences are transforming how consumers interact with products online.

- **Real Estate and Architecture**: VR allows potential buyers to tour properties remotely, while AR enables architects to visualize designs in real-world environments before construction.

- **Industrial and Manufacturing**: AR assists workers in assembling complex machinery by overlaying instructions, while VR is used for training and safety simulations.

8. Ethical Considerations and Challenges

AS AR AND VR TECHNOLOGIES advance, they bring ethical challenges and concerns that must be addressed:

- **Privacy and Data Security**: AR glasses and VR headsets collect vast amounts of user data, raising concerns about privacy, surveillance, and data misuse.

- **Digital Addiction and Mental Health**: Excessive use of immersive experiences may contribute to addiction, social isolation, and potential psychological effects.

- **Content Moderation in the Metaverse**: As social VR spaces grow, issues such as harassment, misinformation, and virtual crimes will require robust moderation and governance frameworks.

- **Accessibility and Inclusion**: Ensuring that AR/VR experiences are accessible to people with disabilities, including visual, auditory, and motor impairments, remains a priority.

9. Conclusion

THE FUTURE OF AR AND VR is filled with limitless possibilities, from hyper-realistic virtual environments to seamless digital overlays on the physical world. Innovations in hardware, AI, cloud computing, and user interfaces are driving AR/VR toward mainstream adoption across industries. As these technologies continue to evolve, ethical considerations and responsible development will be crucial in shaping an inclusive, immersive, and interconnected digital future.

With the integration of AR and VR into everyday life, we are moving towards a world where the boundaries between the physical and digital realms blur, opening new opportunities for communication, creativity, and exploration. The next decade promises a revolutionary shift in how we experience reality—both augmented and virtual.

Ethical Considerations in AR & VR Development

THE RAPID ADVANCEMENT of Augmented Reality (AR) and Virtual Reality (VR) technology brings not only exciting possibilities but also critical ethical considerations. As AR and VR become deeply integrated into entertainment, business, healthcare, education, and everyday life, developers must address a range of ethical concerns, including privacy, security, accessibility, digital well-being, and societal impact. Failing to consider these issues can lead to unintended consequences that undermine trust in AR and VR applications.

1. Privacy and Data Security Concerns

AR AND VR APPLICATIONS collect vast amounts of data, including biometric information, user behavior, environmental mapping, and even eye-tracking data. This level of data collection presents serious privacy risks.

Types of Sensitive Data Collected

- **Personal Identifiable Information (PII):** Name, age, email, location, and other personal details collected through user profiles.

- **Biometric Data:** Eye movements, facial recognition data, and even gait analysis, which can uniquely identify individuals.

- **Environmental Data:** AR devices scan and map physical environments, raising concerns about unauthorized data collection in private spaces.

- **Interaction Data:** VR platforms collect information about user interactions, including movement patterns, preferences, and time spent in different activities.

Potential Privacy Risks

- **Unauthorized Surveillance:** AR glasses and VR headsets could be used to secretly record individuals, raising surveillance concerns.

- **Data Monetization and Profiling:** Companies may use collected data for targeted advertising or sell it to third parties without user consent.

- **Hacking and Data Breaches:** Cyberattacks on AR/VR platforms can expose user data, leading to identity theft or misuse.

Best Practices for Privacy and Security

DEVELOPERS MUST IMPLEMENT strict security measures and transparent privacy policies, including:

- **End-to-End Encryption:** Encrypt user data to prevent unauthorized access.

- **On-Device Processing:** Whenever possible, process sensitive data locally instead of sending it to cloud servers.

- **User Consent and Control:** Provide users with clear options to opt out of data collection.

- **Minimal Data Collection:** Collect only the necessary data to run AR/VR applications effectively.

2. Ethical Challenges of Deep Immersion

VR IS DESIGNED TO BE highly immersive, which raises concerns about its psychological impact on users. The deep engagement in virtual environments can lead to both positive and negative effects.

Mental and Emotional Well-Being

- **VR Addiction:** Some users may develop an unhealthy dependence on virtual worlds, similar to gaming addiction.

- **Desensitization to Violence:** Exposure to violent or disturbing VR experiences could reduce emotional sensitivity to real-world events.

- **Psychological Distress:** Some VR content may induce anxiety, PTSD symptoms, or emotional distress, particularly in highly immersive simulations.

Ethical Responsibility of Developers

- **Content Moderation:** Implement filters and moderation tools to prevent harmful content.

- **Time Management Features:** Encourage users to take breaks and monitor their time spent in VR.

- **Diversity and Inclusion in Content Design:** Ensure that VR experiences represent different perspectives and do not reinforce stereotypes.

3. Ethical AI and Personalization in AR & VR

ARTIFICIAL INTELLIGENCE (AI) plays a crucial role in AR and VR applications, personalizing experiences based on user behavior. However, ethical concerns arise when AI-driven content adaptation leads to biased, manipulative, or harmful experiences.

Algorithmic Bias and Fairness

- **Racial and Gender Bias in AI Models:** If trained on biased datasets, AI systems may produce discriminatory results.

- **AI-Driven Decision Making:** AR/VR platforms using AI for hiring simulations, educational assessments, or security profiling must ensure fairness.

Manipulation and Dark Patterns

SOME AR/VR APPLICATIONS use psychological tricks to manipulate users into making purchases, extending engagement times, or sharing data.

- **Dark UX Patterns:** Intentionally making it difficult for users to exit or change settings (e.g., confusing exit buttons, hidden privacy controls).

- **Emotional Manipulation:** AI-driven virtual assistants or NPCs that manipulate users into making emotional purchases.

- **Gambling-Like Mechanics:** Implementing loot boxes, microtransactions, or other exploitative monetization techniques in VR experiences.

Best Practices for Ethical AI in AR & VR

- **Transparency:** Clearly inform users how AI is being used in applications.
- **Bias Mitigation Strategies:** Continuously audit and improve AI models to remove biases.
- **User Control:** Allow users to opt out of AI-driven personalization.

4. Accessibility and Inclusion in AR & VR

AR AND VR SHOULD BE designed to be inclusive and accessible to users with disabilities, ensuring equal access to immersive technologies.

Challenges Faced by Disabled Users

- **Visual Impairments:** Many AR interfaces rely on visual elements, making it difficult for visually impaired users to navigate.
- **Hearing Impairments:** Lack of subtitles or audio descriptions in VR experiences creates barriers for deaf users.
- **Motor Impairments:** Traditional controllers and gestures may not be usable for people with limited mobility.

Solutions for Inclusive AR & VR

- **Voice Commands and Adaptive Controls:** Implement voice navigation and customizable input methods.

- **Haptic Feedback for the Deaf and Blind:** Provide haptic cues to represent sound-based interactions.

- **Screen Readers and AR Enhancements:** Develop AR overlays with audio descriptions for visually impaired users.

- **Adjustable Comfort Settings:** Allow users to modify color schemes, contrast levels, and text sizes.

5. Ethical Considerations in the Metaverse

AS AR AND VR MERGE into persistent virtual worlds known as the Metaverse, new ethical concerns emerge, including governance, identity, and virtual economies.

Identity and Anonymity

- **Avatar Identity Fraud:** Users can impersonate others, leading to fraud, deception, and cybercrime.

- **Anonymity vs. Accountability:** While anonymity can protect free expression, it also allows for toxic behavior and harassment.

Harassment and Safety in Virtual Spaces

- **Virtual Harassment:** Instances of verbal abuse, stalking, and unwanted interactions in VR spaces require strong moderation.

- **Safe Zones and Reporting Systems:** Developers should integrate blocking, reporting, and AI moderation tools to prevent harassment.

Economic Ethics in the Metaverse

- **Virtual Labor Exploitation:** Some platforms allow users to earn real money through virtual work, raising concerns about fair wages and economic exploitation.

- **Decentralization and Regulation:** As virtual real estate, digital currencies, and NFT-based goods grow in popularity, regulation must ensure ethical trade practices.

6. Environmental Impact of AR & VR

ALTHOUGH AR AND VR reduce physical travel and material waste in some industries, they also have significant environmental impacts.

Energy Consumption

- **VR Data Centers and Cloud Computing:** VR applications rely heavily on cloud processing, increasing energy use.

- **Manufacturing of AR/VR Hardware:** The production of headsets and sensors requires rare materials, contributing to e-waste.

Sustainable Solutions

- **Energy-Efficient Hardware:** Develop AR/VR devices with lower power consumption.

- **Recycling and E-Waste Management:** Encourage recycling programs for outdated AR/VR devices.

7. Conclusion

AS AR AND VR TECHNOLOGIES advance, ethical considerations must remain a priority. From protecting privacy and ensuring accessibility to addressing AI biases and environmental sustainability, developers and policymakers must work together to create a responsible and ethical AR/VR ecosystem. Ethical design and transparent policies will ensure that AR and VR enrich human experiences without causing harm or exploitation.

The Role of AR & VR in the Metaverse

THE METAVERSE IS AN evolving digital ecosystem that blends virtual, augmented, and real-world elements into an interconnected space where users can interact, socialize, work, and engage in digital economies. Augmented Reality (AR) and Virtual Reality (VR) serve as foundational technologies that enable immersive experiences within the Metaverse, transforming the way people interact with digital environments.

As AR and VR technologies advance, they play a crucial role in shaping the Metaverse's infrastructure, accessibility, economy, and user experience. This section explores the various dimensions of AR and VR's role in the Metaverse, from hardware and software to ethics, governance, and future possibilities.

1. The Metaverse and Its Connection to AR & VR

THE CONCEPT OF THE Metaverse is not new, but its realization has accelerated due to advancements in AR and VR. Unlike traditional internet experiences, the Metaverse is immersive, persistent, and interactive.

Key Characteristics of the Metaverse

- **Persistent Digital Worlds** – Unlike conventional apps or games, Metaverse spaces exist continuously, even when users are not present.
- **Interoperability** – Users can move seamlessly between different virtual spaces, maintaining their avatars, assets, and digital identities.
- **User-Generated Content** – AR and VR platforms enable users to create virtual environments, objects, and experiences.
- **Social and Economic Interactions** – The Metaverse supports social engagements, e-commerce, virtual real estate, and digital jobs.

AR vs. VR in the Metaverse

Feature	Augmented Reality (AR)	Virtual Reality (VR)
Accessibility	Accessible via smartphones and AR glasses	Requires headsets for full immersion
Environment	Blends virtual elements into the real world	Entirely virtual, isolating users from the physical world
User Interaction	Enhances real-world experiences	Provides fully immersive digital interactions
Use Cases	Navigation, remote assistance, retail, gaming	Gaming, training, simulation, social interactions

2. AR & VR Technologies Powering the Metaverse

FOR THE METAVERSE TO function as an immersive digital space, AR and VR must overcome several technological challenges. From hardware to software, these advancements drive the future of virtual experiences.

Hardware Innovations

1. **Advanced VR Headsets** – Devices such as the Meta Quest Pro, Apple Vision Pro, and HTC Vive XR Elite incorporate higher resolutions, better field of view (FoV), and improved refresh rates.
2. **AR Smart Glasses** – Companies like Google, Meta, and Apple are developing lightweight, everyday-use AR glasses that seamlessly overlay digital content onto real-world

environments.

3. **Haptic Feedback Devices** – Haptic gloves, bodysuits, and motion sensors enhance the realism of digital interactions, allowing users to "feel" virtual objects.
4. **Eye-Tracking and Facial Recognition** – Eye-tracking improves rendering efficiency (foveated rendering) and enhances avatar expressions in virtual spaces.

Software and Platforms

THE METAVERSE RELIES on software ecosystems that connect users across different AR and VR platforms.

- **Game Engines** – Platforms like Unity and Unreal Engine power most AR and VR Metaverse experiences.

- **Cloud Computing & Edge Computing** – Processing AR/VR content via cloud servers reduces hardware requirements for end users.

- **AI and Machine Learning** – AI personalizes virtual environments, enhances realism, and automates NPC interactions.

```
// Example of AI-driven virtual avatar behavior in the Metaverse using JavaScript

class VirtualAvatar {

constructor(name) {

this.name = name;

this.mood = "neutral";
```

```
}
interact(userEmotion) {
if (userEmotion === "happy") {
this.mood = "smiling";
} else if (userEmotion === "sad") {
this.mood = "concerned";
} else {
this.mood = "neutral";
}
return `Avatar ${this.name} is now ${this.mood}`;
}
}
let avatar = new VirtualAvatar("Neo");
console.log(avatar.interact("happy")); // Output: Avatar Neo is now smiling
```

3. Social and Economic Impact of AR & VR in the Metaverse

AR AND VR EXPAND THE possibilities of human interaction in the Metaverse, creating new opportunities and challenges.

Virtual Social Spaces

- **Immersive Meetings and Events** – Platforms like Meta's Horizon Workrooms enable remote work in VR.

- **Digital Socializing** – Virtual worlds like VRChat and Rec Room provide spaces for social interactions, concerts, and parties.

- **Personalized Avatars** – Users express themselves through customizable avatars that reflect their identity.

The Digital Economy

THE METAVERSE INTEGRATES digital commerce powered by cryptocurrencies, blockchain, and NFTs.

- **Virtual Real Estate** – Platforms like Decentraland allow users to buy, sell, and develop virtual land.

- **Digital Goods and NFTs** – Virtual fashion, skins, and accessories are sold as NFTs, ensuring ownership.

- **Metaverse Employment** – Users can work as virtual architects, event organizers, digital fashion designers, and more.

```
# Example of a simple NFT-based ownership check using blockchain technology

class NFT:

def __init__(self, owner, asset):

self.owner = owner
```

```
self.asset = asset
def transfer(self, new_owner):
self.owner = new_owner
return f"NFT now owned by {new_owner}"
virtual_land = NFT("Alice", "Plot #42 in Decentraland")
print(virtual_land.transfer("Bob")) # Output: NFT now owned by Bob
```

4. Challenges and Ethical Concerns

AS AR AND VR GROW IN the Metaverse, ethical issues and challenges emerge.

Privacy and Surveillance

- **AR Smart Glasses and Data Collection** – Always-on cameras and microphones raise concerns about surveillance and consent.
- **VR Data Privacy** – Motion data, eye tracking, and voice interactions are collected, leading to potential misuse.

Mental and Social Impact

- **Digital Identity Crisis** – Users may struggle to balance virtual and real-world identities.

- **Addiction and Mental Health** – Highly immersive virtual worlds can lead to addiction and social withdrawal.

- **Harassment in Virtual Spaces** – Instances of harassment, bullying, and misinformation need stronger moderation.

Regulation and Governance

- **Lack of Standardization** – There is no universal protocol for Metaverse interoperability.

- **Digital Rights Management** – Ensuring fair digital ownership and preventing counterfeit NFTs.

- **Accessibility Issues** – Many VR applications are not designed for people with disabilities.

---

5. Future of AR & VR in the Metaverse

THE NEXT DECADE WILL see significant improvements in AR and VR as they become integral to the Metaverse.

Next-Generation AR & VR Devices

- **Ultra-Thin AR Glasses** – Expected to replace smartphones for everyday digital interactions.

- **Wireless Brain-Computer Interfaces (BCI)** – Companies like Neuralink are exploring direct neural control of virtual environments.

- **Full-Sensory VR** – Advances in haptic technology, scent simulation, and brain stimulation will make VR more immersive.

AI-Powered Virtual Assistants

AI-DRIVEN AVATARS WILL act as personal assistants, helping users navigate the Metaverse.

Hyper-Realistic Digital Twins

AR WILL ALLOW BUSINESSES to create digital replicas of real-world locations, used for training, simulations, and commerce.

{

"DigitalTwin": {

"location": "London",

"industry": "Retail",

"function": "Simulating customer behavior for optimization"

}

}

---

6. Conclusion

AR AND VR ARE THE BACKBONE of the Metaverse, shaping how users interact with digital spaces, conduct business, and engage in social activities. While the potential is limitless, ethical concerns, accessibility, and technological challenges must be addressed for the Metaverse to reach its full potential. As AR and VR continue to evolve, they will redefine the boundaries of human experience, blurring the lines between the real and the virtual.

Preparing for the Next Generation of AR & VR

THE NEXT GENERATION of Augmented Reality (AR) and Virtual Reality (VR) will redefine how we interact with digital and physical spaces. As hardware, software, and artificial intelligence (AI) evolve, developers, businesses, and consumers must prepare for a more immersive and interconnected future. The transition to this next phase requires advancements in several key areas, including technological infrastructure, ethical considerations, user experience design, and industry-wide standardization.

This section explores the essential steps in preparing for the next generation of AR & VR, covering hardware developments, software evolution, ethical responsibilities, and new business opportunities.

---

1. The Evolution of AR & VR Hardware

THE FUTURE OF AR & VR depends on major improvements in hardware. Current headsets are bulky, expensive, and limited by computational power. However, the next generation of devices aims to overcome these challenges.

Key Areas of Hardware Development

1. **Lightweight, All-Day Wearable AR Glasses**

   ○ Future AR glasses will be as comfortable as regular eyeglasses.

○ Companies like Apple, Meta, and Google are working on AR glasses that integrate seamlessly with daily life.

2. **Next-Gen VR Headsets with 8K Resolution & HDR Displays**

○ Higher-resolution displays will eliminate the screen-door effect.

○ Improved refresh rates (120Hz+) and wider field of view (FOV) will enhance immersion.

3. **Wireless & Cloud-Connected VR**

○ Cloud rendering will enable high-end graphics on lightweight headsets.

○ 5G and Wi-Fi 6 will reduce latency for real-time VR streaming.

4. **Full-Body Haptic Suits & Sensory Feedback**

○ Wearable devices will provide realistic touch sensations.

○ Advanced haptics will simulate temperature, pressure, and movement.

Hardware Challenges & Solutions

Challenge	Solution
High power consumption	Energy-efficient processors & edge computing
Motion sickness	AI-powered real-time motion prediction
Cost barriers	Open-source development & mass production

2. Software & Development Tools for Next-Gen AR & VR

THE SUCCESS OF NEXT-generation AR & VR depends on software advancements that make development faster, easier, and more scalable.

Emerging Development Tools

- **AI-Driven Development Frameworks** – AI will assist in generating 3D models, physics simulations, and virtual environments.
- **No-Code & Low-Code Platforms** – Democratizing AR/VR development by allowing non-programmers to create immersive experiences.
- **Cross-Platform Development Kits** – Standardized SDKs will allow AR & VR applications to run seamlessly across devices.

```
// EXAMPLE: A SIMPLE AR object placement using WebXR API

function placeVirtualObject(scene, position) {
```

```
const object = new THREE.Mesh(
new THREE.BoxGeometry(1, 1, 1),
new THREE.MeshStandardMaterial({ color: "blue" })
);
object.position.set(position.x, position.y, position.z);
scene.add(object);
}
```

Next-Generation Rendering & AI Integration

- **Real-Time Ray Tracing in VR** – Enhancing graphical realism through accurate lighting simulations.
- **Procedural World Generation** – AI will create dynamic environments based on user interactions.
- **AI-Powered Avatars** – Virtual assistants and NPCs will adapt to user emotions and behavior.

```
# AI-POWERED NPC BEHAVIOR simulation
class VirtualNPC:
def __init__(self, name):
self.name = name
self.mood = "neutral"
def respond_to_user(self, user_emotion):
```

```
responses = {
"happy": "I'm glad to see you're in a good mood!",
"sad": "I'm here to help if you need support.",
"angry": "Let's try to solve this together."
}
return responses.get(user_emotion, "Hello, how can I assist you today?")
npc = VirtualNPC("Echo")
print(npc.respond_to_user("happy"))
```

3. Ethical & Privacy Considerations in the Next Generation of AR & VR

AS AR & VR BECOME MORE integrated into daily life, ethical considerations must be addressed to ensure user trust and safety.

User Data Protection & Privacy

- **AR & VR devices collect biometric data, eye-tracking information, and movement patterns.**
- **Secure encryption and on-device processing should be prioritized to prevent data leaks.**

AI Bias & Ethical Design

- **Algorithmic bias in virtual simulations must be actively mitigated.**

- **Diverse datasets should be used to train AI models in AR & VR applications.**

Moderation in Virtual Spaces

- **Ensuring safety in the Metaverse will require AI-driven content moderation.**

- **Virtual harassment and abuse prevention measures should be a priority.**

---

4. Preparing Industries for Next-Gen AR & VR

THE IMPACT OF AR & VR will extend beyond entertainment into various industries. Businesses and governments must prepare for digital transformation.

Education & Training

- **Virtual Classrooms** – Interactive learning environments will replace traditional teaching methods.

- **Corporate Training Simulations** – Employees will use VR for skill-based training in medicine, engineering, and military applications.

Healthcare & Therapy

- **VR for Pain Management** – Immersive VR environments can reduce pain perception in patients.

- **AR-Assisted Surgeries** – Surgeons will use AR overlays for precision procedures.

Retail & E-Commerce

- **Virtual Try-On Technology** – Customers will use AR to preview products before purchasing.

- **Metaverse Shopping Malls** – Brands will set up digital storefronts within virtual spaces.

```
{
"VirtualStore": {
"brand": "XYZ Fashion",
"location": "Metaverse",
"features": ["3D try-on", "NFT clothing", "Live customer support"]
}
}
```

5. Business & Monetization Strategies for AR & VR

AS AR & VR ADOPTION grows, businesses must prepare for new monetization strategies.

Subscription-Based AR/VR Services

- **Cloud VR Gaming Platforms** – Monthly subscriptions for high-end VR content streaming.

- **Enterprise AR Solutions** – Businesses will subscribe to AR tools for training and productivity.

Virtual Property & NFT Marketplaces

- **Virtual Real Estate Ownership** – Users will buy and rent virtual land for digital experiences.

- **NFT-Backed Digital Goods** – Unique virtual items will be sold as NFTs in AR & VR environments.

Advertising in AR & VR

- **AR-Based Location Advertising** – Local businesses will place AR advertisements within real-world environments.

- **Product Placement in VR Worlds** – Brands will integrate products into immersive experiences.

```
// EXAMPLE OF AR ADVERTISING placement

function displayAd(location, content) {

let adElement = document.createElement("div");

adElement.innerText = content;

adElement.style.position = "absolute";

adElement.style.top = location.y + "px";

adElement.style.left = location.x + "px";

document.body.appendChild(adElement);
```

```
}
displayAd({ x: 100, y: 50 }, "Try our new VR headset!");
```

6. Conclusion

THE NEXT GENERATION of AR & VR will revolutionize industries, reshape human interactions, and create new digital economies. Preparing for this future requires advancements in hardware, software, and ethical considerations. Developers, businesses, and governments must collaborate to ensure that AR & VR technologies are accessible, secure, and beneficial for all users.

By embracing emerging technologies, maintaining ethical transparency, and creating sustainable business models, the next wave of AR & VR will transform society in unprecedented ways. The future is not just about virtual worlds—it's about seamlessly integrating digital and physical realities to create meaningful and impactful experiences.

Chapter 11: Appendices

Glossary of Terms

Augmented Reality (AR)

AUGMENTED REALITY (AR) is a technology that overlays digital content onto the real world using devices such as smartphones, tablets, or AR glasses. Unlike Virtual Reality, AR does not create a fully immersive environment but enhances the physical world with digital elements.

Virtual Reality (VR)

VIRTUAL REALITY (VR) is an immersive technology that places users in a fully digital environment, blocking out the real world. VR experiences are typically accessed using headsets like the Oculus Quest, HTC Vive, or PlayStation VR.

Mixed Reality (MR)

MIXED REALITY (MR) is a blend of AR and VR where digital objects are anchored to the real world and interact with it in real time. Microsoft HoloLens is a prominent MR device.

Extended Reality (XR)

EXTENDED REALITY (XR) is an umbrella term that encompasses AR, VR, and MR technologies.

Spatial Computing

SPATIAL COMPUTING REFERS to the ability of digital systems to interact and compute within 3D space, allowing for realistic interactions with virtual objects.

Six Degrees of Freedom (6DOF)

6DOF REFERS TO MOVEMENT in three-dimensional space with six possible axes: forward/backward, up/down, left/right, and rotation along three axes (pitch, yaw, and roll).

Three Degrees of Freedom (3DOF)

3DOF REFERS TO MOVEMENT that only allows rotational tracking without positional tracking, common in lower-end VR headsets.

Field of View (FoV)

FOV IS THE EXTENT OF the observable environment seen through an AR or VR device, measured in degrees.

Latency

LATENCY IS THE DELAY between a user's action and the corresponding system response, crucial in AR and VR applications to avoid motion sickness.

Refresh Rate

THE REFRESH RATE IS the number of times per second (measured in Hz) a display updates its image. Higher refresh rates reduce motion blur and improve immersion.

Rendering Pipeline

THE RENDERING PIPELINE refers to the series of steps a system takes to convert 3D models and textures into a final image displayed in AR/VR.

Foveated Rendering

A TECHNIQUE THAT RENDERS at high resolution only in the area where the user is looking, reducing computational load.

Depth Perception

DEPTH PERCEPTION IS the ability of a system to understand distances between objects using stereoscopic vision, LiDAR, or depth sensors.

Haptic Feedback

HAPTIC FEEDBACK REFERS to tactile sensations provided by devices such as controllers or gloves to simulate physical interactions in AR and VR.

Inside-Out Tracking

A TRACKING SYSTEM WHERE cameras or sensors on the AR/VR headset determine position without external devices.

Outside-In Tracking

A TRACKING METHOD THAT relies on external sensors or cameras to track a user's position.

Positional Tracking

A TECHNOLOGY THAT TRACKS a user's position in space, essential for VR experiences that support movement.

Hand Tracking

HAND TRACKING ENABLES users to interact with virtual environments using their hands instead of controllers, typically using cameras or depth sensors.

Eye Tracking

A FEATURE IN ADVANCED AR/VR headsets that monitors eye movements to improve interaction and optimize rendering.

Gaze-Based Interaction

A METHOD OF INTERACTING with virtual elements by looking at them instead of using controllers or hand gestures.

Room-Scale VR

A VR SETUP THAT ALLOWS users to move freely within a defined space, typically requiring 6DOF tracking.

Passthrough AR

A FEATURE IN SOME VR headsets that allows users to see the real world through built-in cameras while wearing the headset.

Light Field Display

A DISPLAY TECHNOLOGY that simulates how light interacts with objects to create more realistic depth perception in AR and VR.

SLAM (Simultaneous Localization and Mapping)

A TECHNOLOGY USED IN AR applications to map an environment and track the position of a device in real time.

Object Occlusion

A FEATURE THAT ALLOWS digital objects in AR to be blocked by real-world objects, creating a more realistic experience.

Occlusion Culling

A RENDERING OPTIMIZATION technique that prevents the system from rendering objects not visible to the user.

Raycasting

A TECHNIQUE USED TO determine the intersection of a virtual ray with objects in a 3D scene, commonly used for user interactions.

World Anchors

PERSISTENT POINTS IN space that AR applications use to position virtual objects reliably in the real world.

Plane Detection

A FEATURE IN AR THAT identifies flat surfaces like tables and floors for placing virtual objects.

Marker-Based AR

AN AR TECHNOLOGY THAT relies on predefined visual markers (e.g., QR codes) to trigger the display of digital content.

Markerless AR

AN AR APPROACH THAT does not require predefined markers and instead uses SLAM or other techniques to place digital objects.

AR Cloud

A SHARED DIGITAL REPRESENTATION of the real world that multiple AR users can interact with in real time.

Volumetric Capture

A TECHNIQUE FOR CAPTURING a 3D representation of a person or object for use in AR/VR experiences.

Photogrammetry

A TECHNIQUE THAT CREATES 3D models by processing multiple images taken from different angles.

VR Locomotion

METHODS OF MOVING WITHIN a VR environment, including teleportation, smooth movement, and arm-swinging.

Comfort Mode

SETTINGS DESIGNED TO reduce motion sickness, such as limiting camera movement or reducing acceleration.

Room Setup

THE PROCESS OF CONFIGURING a VR space by defining the play area, boundary, and tracking points.

SDK (Software Development Kit)

A COLLECTION OF TOOLS, libraries, and documentation that enables developers to build AR/VR applications.

OpenXR

AN OPEN STANDARD FOR AR/VR development that allows applications to work across different hardware platforms.

WebXR

A WEB-BASED STANDARD for creating AR/VR experiences that run in browsers without requiring dedicated applications.

Metaverse

A PERSISTENT, SHARED digital universe where users can interact with virtual objects, environments, and other users.

Persistent AR

A FEATURE THAT ALLOWS AR experiences to retain state across multiple sessions, ensuring virtual objects remain in place.

XR Input System

A FRAMEWORK FOR HANDLING inputs from various AR/ VR controllers, hand tracking, and eye tracking devices.

Gesture Recognition

A TECHNOLOGY THAT ALLOWS AR/VR systems to interpret user gestures as inputs.

Virtual Production

A FILMMAKING TECHNIQUE that combines real-time AR/VR elements with traditional filmmaking methods.

Digital Twin

A VIRTUAL REPRESENTATION of a physical object or environment used for simulations and analysis.

Holography

A TECHNOLOGY THAT CREATES three-dimensional visual representations of objects without requiring AR/VR headsets.

Edge Computing in AR/VR

PROCESSING AR/VR DATA on edge devices instead of relying solely on cloud computing to reduce latency.

Cloud Rendering

A TECHNIQUE WHERE GRAPHICS processing is offloaded to cloud servers to deliver high-quality AR/VR visuals on lower-end devices.

Multi-User AR/VR

EXPERIENCES WHERE MULTIPLE users can interact with the same AR/VR environment simultaneously.

XR Accessibility

DESIGN CONSIDERATIONS that ensure AR/VR applications are usable by people with disabilities.

Spatial Audio

A SOUND DESIGN TECHNIQUE that places audio sources in 3D space to enhance immersion in AR/VR environments.

Holographic Displays

DISPLAYS CAPABLE OF projecting 3D images that can be viewed without AR/VR headsets.

AR Glasses

WEARABLE DEVICES THAT overlay digital content onto the real world, such as Microsoft HoloLens or Magic Leap.

VR Gloves

WEARABLE GLOVES EQUIPPED with sensors to provide tactile feedback and hand tracking in VR applications.

Presence

THE PSYCHOLOGICAL FEELING of "being there" in a virtual environment, a key factor in immersion.

AR Filters

OVERLAYS APPLIED TO real-world camera feeds, commonly seen in social media apps like Snapchat and Instagram.

Mixed Reality Portal

A FEATURE IN SOME VR headsets that allows users to step between virtual and real-world spaces seamlessly.

This glossary provides a foundational understanding of the key terms and concepts in AR and VR development, helping developers, designers, and enthusiasts navigate the rapidly evolving XR landscape.

Resources for Further Learning

Books on AR & VR Development

1. **"Learning Augmented Reality Development" by Claude Panozzo**
   A beginner-friendly introduction to AR, covering ARKit and ARCore with practical examples.
2. **"Unity Virtual Reality Projects" by Jonathan Linowes**
   Focuses on VR development using Unity, including locomotion techniques and game mechanics.
3. **"Augmented Human: How Technology Is Shaping the New Reality" by Helen Papagiannis**
   Explores how AR is changing various industries and its future implications.
4. **"Mastering Augmented Reality Development" by Joseph Hocking**
   Covers advanced AR development topics, including 3D tracking, spatial mapping, and AR business applications.
5. **"The Infinite Retina: Spatial Computing, Augmented Reality, and How a Collision of New Technologies is Bringing about the Next Tech Revolution" by Irena Cronin and Robert Scoble**
   A deep dive into spatial computing and the future of AR/VR in enterprise solutions.

Online Courses and Tutorials

Beginner-Friendly Courses

- **Coursera - Introduction to Augmented Reality and ARCore[1] (by Google AR & VR)**

  Teaches the fundamentals of AR development using ARCore.

- **Udacity - VR Foundations**

  A great introduction to VR development covering Unity and Oculus VR SDKs.

- **Pluralsight - Getting Started with Augmented Reality Development**

  Covers marker-based and markerless AR applications.

Intermediate to Advanced Courses

- **Udemy - Mastering ARKit for iOS**

  Focuses on ARKit with Swift, including real-world mapping and object detection.

- **edX - Virtual Reality App Development**

  Explores advanced VR development topics such as physics simulation and AI integration.

- **XR Bootcamp[2]**

---

1. https://www.coursera.org/learn/ar

Offers professional-level courses on XR development with a focus on industry applications.

Open-Source Frameworks and SDKs

Augmented Reality SDKs

- **ARKit**[3] (iOS)

Apple's AR development kit supporting object tracking, LiDAR, and 3D object placement.

- **ARCore** (Android)

Google's AR SDK with motion tracking, environmental understanding, and light estimation.

- **Vuforia**

A widely used AR SDK with advanced object recognition and tracking capabilities.

- **EasyAR**[4]

A lightweight AR engine optimized for mobile applications.

Virtual Reality SDKs

- **OpenXR**

---

2. https://xrbootcamp.com/

3. https://developer.apple.com/augmented-reality/

4. https://www.easyar.com/

A cross-platform XR standard supporting multiple VR and AR headsets.

- **Oculus SDK**

Meta's official SDK for building VR applications on Oculus devices.

- **SteamVR**

Valve's SDK for developing VR applications compatible with various headsets.

AR & VR Development Tools

- **Unity**[5]

One of the most popular game engines for AR and VR development.

- **Unreal Engine**[6]

A high-performance engine used for photorealistic VR experiences.

- **Blender**[7]

A free and open-source 3D modeling software used to create assets for AR/VR.

- **MRTK (Mixed Reality Toolkit)**[8]

---

5. https://unity.com/

6. https://www.unrealengine.com/

7. https://www.blender.org/

8. https://github.com/microsoft/MixedRealityToolkit-Unity

Microsoft's open-source toolkit for building Mixed Reality applications.

- **Three.js**[9]

A JavaScript library for rendering 3D graphics in a web-based AR/VR environment.

- **A-Frame**[10]

A web framework for building VR experiences using HTML and JavaScript.

Coding Resources and Documentation

Official Documentation

- **ARKit Developer Documentation**[11]
- **ARCore Developer Guide**
- **Vuforia Developer Portal**
- **Oculus Developer Documentation**
- **SteamVR API Reference**[12]

Code Repositories and Sample Projects

- **GitHub - Unity-ARKit-Plugin**[13]

---

9. https://threejs.org/
10. https://aframe.io/
11. https://developer.apple.com/documentation/arkit/
12. https://github.com/ValveSoftware/openvr/wiki
13. https://github.com/Unity-Technologies/arfoundation-samples

- **Google AR Experiments**
- **Microsoft Mixed Reality Samples**[14]

Example Code Snippets

BASIC AR OBJECT PLACEMENT in ARKit (Swift)

```
import ARKit
import SceneKit
class ViewController: UIViewController, ARSCNViewDelegate {
@IBOutlet var sceneView: ARSCNView!
override func viewDidLoad() {
super.viewDidLoad()
sceneView.delegate = self
sceneView.scene = SCNScene()
}
override func viewWillAppear(_ animated: Bool) {
super.viewWillAppear(animated)
let configuration = ARWorldTrackingConfiguration()
sceneView.session.run(configuration)
}
func addObject(at position: SCNVector3) {
```

14. https://github.com/microsoft/MixedRealityToolkit-Unity

```
let sphere = SCNSphere(radius: 0.1)
let material = SCNMaterial()
material.diffuse.contents = UIColor.blue
sphere.materials = [material]
let node = SCNNode(geometry: sphere)
node.position = position
sceneView.scene.rootNode.addChildNode(node)
}
}
```

Basic VR Scene in Three.js

```
import * as THREE from 'three';
import { VRButton } from 'three/examples/jsm/webxr/VRButton.js';
const scene = new THREE.Scene();
const camera = new THREE.PerspectiveCamera(75, window.innerWidth / window.innerHeight, 0.1, 1000);
const renderer = new THREE.WebGLRenderer();
renderer.xr.enabled = true;
document.body.appendChild(VRButton.createButton(renderer));
document.body.appendChild(renderer.domElement);
const geometry = new THREE.BoxGeometry();
```

```
const material = new THREE.MeshBasicMaterial({ color: 0x00ff00
});

const cube = new THREE.Mesh(geometry, material);

scene.add(cube);

camera.position.z = 5;

renderer.setAnimationLoop(() => {

renderer.render(scene, camera);

});
```

AR & VR Communities and Forums

- **Augmented Reality Developers Slack**
- **Oculus Developer Forum**
- **AR/VR Stack Exchange**[15]
- **r/AR_MR_XR**[16]
- **VR Developers Discord**

Podcasts and YouTube Channels

- **Voices of VR Podcast**[17]
- **AR Show with Jason McDowall**[18]
- **UploadVR YouTube Channel**[19]

---

15. https://ar.stackexchange.com/

16. https://www.reddit.com/r/AR_MR_XR/

17. https://voicesofvr.com/

18. https://thearshow.com/

- **CNET VR Channel**[20]
- **Meta Reality Labs YouTube**[21]

THIS SECTION SERVES as a comprehensive guide to learning and advancing in AR and VR development, providing books, courses, tools, communities, and code examples.

Sample Projects and Code Snippets

Introduction to Sample Projects

DEVELOPING AR AND VR applications requires a combination of theoretical knowledge and practical implementation. This section includes sample projects demonstrating key concepts in AR and VR development. Each project is designed to highlight essential features, including object placement, user interaction, motion tracking, and environment mapping.

Project 1: Simple AR Object Placement (ARKit - Swift)

Overview

THIS PROJECT ALLOWS users to place a virtual 3D object in the real world using ARKit and SceneKit. The object will appear where the user taps on the screen.

Prerequisites

- Xcode

---

19. https://www.youtube.com/c/UploadVR/

20. https://www.youtube.com/c/CNETVR/

21. https://www.youtube.com/c/OculusDevelopers/

- ARKit-compatible iOS device
- Swift programming knowledge

Implementation

Step 1: Set Up the AR Scene

```
IMPORT UIKIT

import ARKit

class ViewController: UIViewController, ARSCNViewDelegate {

@IBOutlet var sceneView: ARSCNView!

override func viewDidLoad() {

super.viewDidLoad()

sceneView.delegate = self

sceneView.scene = SCNScene()

let tapGesture = UITapGestureRecognizer(target: self, action: #selector(handleTap))

sceneView.addGestureRecognizer(tapGesture)

}

override func viewWillAppear(_ animated: Bool) {

super.viewWillAppear(animated)

let configuration = ARWorldTrackingConfiguration()

sceneView.session.run(configuration)
```

```
}

@objc func handleTap(gestureRecognize: UITapGestureRecognizer) {

let touchLocation = gestureRecognize.location(in: sceneView)

let hitTestResults = sceneView.hitTest(touchLocation, types: .featurePoint)

if let hitResult = hitTestResults.first {

placeObject(at: hitResult.worldTransform)

}

}

func placeObject(at transform: simd_float4x4) {

let objectNode = SCNNode(geometry: SCNSphere(radius: 0.05))

objectNode.geometry?.firstMaterial?.diffuse.contents = UIColor.red

objectNode.simdTransform = transform

sceneView.scene.rootNode.addChildNode(objectNode)

}

}
```

Project 2: Basic VR Environment with Movement (Unity - C#)

Overview

THIS VR PROJECT CREATES a basic virtual environment where users can move around using a VR controller and interact with objects.

Prerequisites

- Unity
- Oculus or SteamVR setup
- VR-ready PC

Implementation

Step 1: Setting Up the Scene

1. Create a new Unity project and import the **XR Interaction Toolkit** package.
2. Add an **XR Rig** from the XR Interaction Toolkit to the scene.
3. Set up movement controls.

Step 2: Implementing VR Movement

```
USING UNITYENGINE;

using UnityEngine.XR;

using UnityEngine.XR.Interaction.Toolkit;
```

```
public class VRMovement : MonoBehaviour
{
public XRNode inputSource;
private Vector2 inputAxis;
public float speed = 2.0f;
private CharacterController characterController;
void Start()
{
characterController = GetComponent<CharacterController>();
}
void Update()
{
InputDevice device = InputDevices.GetDeviceAtXRNode(inputSource);
device.TryGetFeatureValue(CommonUsages.primary2DAxis, out inputAxis);
Vector3 moveDirection = transform.right * inputAxis.x + transform.forward * inputAxis.y;
characterController.Move(moveDirection * speed * Time.deltaTime);
}
}
```

Project 3: Hand Tracking in VR (Oculus - Unity)

Overview

THIS PROJECT IMPLEMENTS Oculus Quest's hand tracking to interact with virtual objects.

Prerequisites

- Oculus Quest
- Unity
- Oculus SDK

Implementation

Step 1: Enable Hand Tracking

1. Go to **Oculus Settings → Enable Hand Tracking**
2. Add **OVRHandPrefab** to the scene

Step 2: Detect Hand Gestures

```
USING UNITYENGINE;

using OculusSampleFramework;

public class HandTracking : MonoBehaviour

{

public OVRHand rightHand;

public OVRHand leftHand;
```

```
void Update()
{
if
(rightHand.GetFingerIsPinching(OVRHand.HandFinger.Index))
{
Debug.Log("Right hand index finger pinch detected!");
}
if (leftHand.GetFingerIsPinching(OVRHand.HandFinger.Index))
{
Debug.Log("Left hand index finger pinch detected!");
}
}
}
```

Project 4: Multiplayer VR Environment (Photon - Unity)

Overview

THIS PROJECT SETS UP a basic multiplayer VR environment using Photon Networking.

Prerequisites

- Photon Unity Networking (PUN)

- Unity
- VR setup

Implementation

Step 1: Setting Up Photon

1. Import **Photon PUN** package
2. Connect to Photon network

```
USING PHOTON.PUN;

using UnityEngine;

public class NetworkManager : MonoBehaviourPunCallbacks

{

void Start()

{

PhotonNetwork.ConnectUsingSettings();

}

public override void OnConnectedToMaster()

{

Debug.Log("Connected to Photon Server");

PhotonNetwork.JoinLobby();

}

}
```

Step 2: Instantiate VR Players

```
USING PHOTON.PUN;
using UnityEngine;
public class VRPlayerSpawner : MonoBehaviour
{
public GameObject vrPlayerPrefab;
void Start()
{
PhotonNetwork.Instantiate(vrPlayerPrefab.name, Vector3.zero, Quaternion.identity);
}
}
```

Project 5: AI-Powered AR Object Recognition (Python - OpenCV)

Overview

THIS AR PROJECT DETECTS objects using AI and places relevant AR content over them.

Prerequisites

- OpenCV
- TensorFlow

- ARCore

Implementation

Step 1: Load Pretrained Object Detection Model

```
IMPORT CV2
import tensorflow as tf
import numpy as np
model = tf.keras.models.load_model("object_detection_model.h5")
def detect_objects(frame):
img_resized = cv2.resize(frame, (224, 224))
img_array = np.expand_dims(img_resized, axis=0)
predictions = model.predict(img_array)
return predictions
```

Step 2: Integrate with AR

```
FUNC OVERLAYAROBJECT(detectedObject: String) {
let objectNode = SCNNode()
if detectedObject == "Chair" {
objectNode.geometry = SCNBox(width: 0.3, height: 0.5, length: 0.3, chamferRadius: 0.02)
objectNode.geometry?.firstMaterial?.diffuse.contents = UIColor.brown
```

```
}
sceneView.scene.rootNode.addChildNode(objectNode)
}
```

Conclusion

THESE SAMPLE PROJECTS cover fundamental and advanced AR/VR development techniques, from object placement to AI integration and multiplayer VR environments. They provide a strong foundation for building real-world AR/VR applications while exploring various SDKs, tools, and programming languages.

API Reference Guide

Introduction to AR & VR APIs

APPLICATION PROGRAMMING Interfaces (APIs) play a crucial role in AR & VR development by providing a structured way to interact with hardware, sensors, and graphics engines. This section provides a detailed reference for key APIs used in AR & VR development, including their functions, usage, and code examples.

1. AR APIs

1.1 ARKit (iOS)

Overview

ARKIT IS APPLE'S AR framework for iOS devices, enabling AR experiences with object tracking, world mapping, and face recognition.

Key Features

- **World tracking** (using SLAM for position tracking)
- **Plane detection** (detects surfaces like floors and tables)
- **Object detection** (recognizes predefined 3D objects)
- **Face tracking** (applies AR effects to user faces)

Example: Placing an AR Object in ARKit

```
IMPORT ARKIT

import SceneKit

class ViewController: UIViewController, ARSCNViewDelegate {

@IBOutlet var sceneView: ARSCNView!

override func viewDidLoad() {

super.viewDidLoad()

sceneView.delegate = self

sceneView.scene = SCNScene()

let tapGesture = UITapGestureRecognizer(target: self, action: #selector(handleTap))

sceneView.addGestureRecognizer(tapGesture)

}

override func viewWillAppear(_ animated: Bool) {

super.viewWillAppear(animated)
```

```
let configuration = ARWorldTrackingConfiguration()
sceneView.session.run(configuration)
}
@objc func handleTap(gestureRecognize: UITapGestureRecognizer) {
let touchLocation = gestureRecognize.location(in: sceneView)
let hitTestResults = sceneView.hitTest(touchLocation, types: .featurePoint)
if let hitResult = hitTestResults.first {
let sphere = SCNSphere(radius: 0.1)
let material = SCNMaterial()
material.diffuse.contents = UIColor.blue
sphere.materials = [material]
let node = SCNNode(geometry: sphere)
node.simdTransform = hitResult.worldTransform
sceneView.scene.rootNode.addChildNode(node)
}
}
}
```

1.2 ARCore (Android)

Overview

ARCORE IS GOOGLE'S AR SDK, providing AR capabilities to Android devices.

Key Features

- **Motion tracking** (tracks device position relative to real-world objects)
- **Environmental understanding** (detects and interacts with real-world surfaces)
- **Light estimation** (adjusts AR object lighting to match real-world conditions)

Example: Detecting a Plane in ARCore

```
VAL ARFRAGMENT = SUPPORTFRAGMENTMANAGER.findFragmentById(R.id.ux_fragme
as ArFragment

arFragment.setOnTapArPlaneListener { hitResult, _, _ ->

val anchor = hitResult.createAnchor()

val anchorNode = AnchorNode(anchor)

anchorNode.setParent(arFragment.arSceneView.scene)

val sphere = ShapeFactory.makeSphere(0.1f, Vector3(0f, 0.1f, 0f),
MaterialFactory.makeOpaqueWithColor(this,
Color(android.graphics.Color.BLUE)))
```

```
val node = Node()

node.setParent(anchorNode)

node.renderable = sphere

}
```

2. VR APIs

2.1 OpenXR

Overview

OPENXR IS A CROSS-PLATFORM API that standardizes VR and AR development.

Key Features

- **Multi-device compatibility** (supports Oculus, SteamVR, and Microsoft MR)
- **Efficient rendering pipeline** (optimized for high-performance VR applications)
- **Haptic feedback support** (integrates vibration feedback in VR experiences)

Example: Setting Up an OpenXR Session

```
XRSESSIONCREATEINFO sessionInfo = {};

sessionInfo.type = XR_TYPE_SESSION_CREATE_INFO;

sessionInfo.next = NULL;
```

```
sessionInfo.systemId = systemId;
sessionInfo.createFlags = 0;
sessionInfo.enabledExtensionCount = 0;
sessionInfo.enabledExtensionNames = NULL;
XrResult result = xrCreateSession(instance, &sessionInfo, &session);
if (result == XR_SUCCESS) {
printf("OpenXR session created successfully.\n");
}
```

2.2 Oculus SDK

Overview

OCULUS SDK PROVIDES tools for building VR applications for Meta Quest and Rift.

Key Features

- **Hand tracking** (detects gestures and hand movements)
- **Positional tracking** (enables 6DOF movement)
- **Multi-user VR experiences** (supports social VR interactions)

Example: Initializing Oculus SDK in Unity

```
USING OCULUS.PLATFORM;
```

```
using Oculus.Platform.Models;
using UnityEngine;
void Start()
{
Core.Initialize();
Users.GetLoggedInUser().OnComplete(HandleUserCallback);
}
void HandleUserCallback(Message<User> message)
{
if (!message.IsError)
{
Debug.Log("User logged in: " + message.Data.OculusID);
}
}
```

3. Additional APIs for AR & VR

3.1 Microsoft Mixed Reality Toolkit (MRTK)

- Provides **hand tracking**, **eye tracking**, and **spatial mapping** for HoloLens and Mixed Reality headsets.
- Supports Unity integration.

```
USING MICROSOFT.MIXEDREALITY.Toolkit.Input;
```

```
void Update()

{

var hand = HandJointUtils.FindHand(Handedness.Right);

if (hand != null)

{

Debug.Log("Right hand detected!");

}

}
```

3.2 Vuforia

- Focuses on **image recognition** and **marker-based AR.**
- Supports integration with Unity.

```
USING VUFORIA;

void Start()

{

ObjectTracker objectTracker = TrackerManager.Instance.GetTracker<ObjectTracker>();

objectTracker.Start();

}
```

4. Web-Based AR & VR APIs

4.1 WebXR API

- Enables AR & VR experiences in web browsers without requiring an app.

```
IF (NAVIGATOR.XR) {
navigator.xr.requestSession('immersive-vr').then(session => {
console.log("VR session started");
});
}
```

4.2 A-Frame (for WebXR Development)

- Simplifies VR development using HTML and JavaScript.

```
<A-SCENE>
<a-box position="0 1.5 -3" color="blue"></a-box>
</a-scene>
```

5. Choosing the Right API

Feature	ARKit	ARCore	OpenXR	Oculus SDK	WebXR
iOS Compatibility	◈	◈	◈	◈	◈
Android Compatibility	◈	◈	◈	◈	◈
Cross-Platform	◈	◈	◈	◈	◈
Marker-Based AR	◈	◈	◈	◈	◈
Hand Tracking	◈	◈	◈	◈	◈
VR Support	◈	◈	◈	◈	◈

Conclusion

APIS FORM THE BACKBONE of AR and VR development. Whether developing AR apps for iOS with ARKit, creating cross-platform VR experiences with OpenXR, or leveraging WebXR for browser-based experiences, developers have multiple options to build immersive applications. This reference guide provides a starting point for integrating these APIs into AR/VR projects.

Frequently Asked Questions

General Questions About AR & VR

What is the difference between AR, VR, and MR?

- **Augmented Reality (AR):** Overlays digital content onto the real world using devices like smartphones, tablets, and AR glasses.

- **Virtual Reality (VR):** Creates a fully immersive digital environment that replaces the real world, requiring a VR headset.

- **Mixed Reality (MR):** A combination of AR and VR where digital objects interact with the real world in real time (e.g., Microsoft HoloLens).

Do I need a powerful computer to develop AR & VR applications?

- **For AR Development:** Mobile AR applications can be developed on mid-range computers, but testing requires an AR-supported smartphone or tablet.

- **For VR Development:** A powerful computer with a high-end GPU is required for desktop VR development (e.g., Oculus Rift, HTC Vive).

- **Standalone VR headsets:** Devices like the Oculus Quest 2 do not require a PC but have hardware limitations compared to PC-based VR.

Development and Programming

Which programming languages are used for AR & VR development?

- **C# (Unity):** Widely used for AR & VR applications, supported by Unity.

- **C++ (Unreal Engine):** Used for high-performance VR applications, especially in Unreal Engine.
- **Swift (ARKit):** Used for iOS-based AR development.
- **Kotlin/Java (ARCore):** Used for Android-based AR applications.
- **JavaScript (WebXR, Three.js, A-Frame):** Used for web-based AR & VR experiences.

What is the best game engine for AR & VR development?

- **Unity:** Best for cross-platform development, supports both AR & VR, widely used in the industry.
- **Unreal Engine:** Offers high-fidelity graphics, preferred for AAA VR games and simulations.
- **Godot Engine:** Open-source alternative for lightweight AR & VR projects.

How do I get started with AR development?

1. **Choose an AR SDK:**
   - ARKit (iOS)
   - ARCore (Android)
   - Vuforia (Marker-based AR)
2. **Set up a development environment:**

○ Use Unity with AR Foundation for cross-platform AR apps.

○ Use Xcode for ARKit and Android Studio for ARCore.

3. **Start with a simple project:**

○ Place a 3D object in AR space.

○ Implement touch interactions.

EXAMPLE: **Basic AR Object Placement (Unity - C#)**

```
using UnityEngine;

using UnityEngine.XR.ARFoundation;

using UnityEngine.XR.ARSubsystems;

public class ARObjectPlacement : MonoBehaviour

{

public GameObject objectPrefab;

private ARRaycastManager raycastManager;

void Start()

{

raycastManager = GetComponent<ARRaycastManager>();

}

void Update()

{
```

```
if (Input.touchCount > 0)
{
Touch touch = Input.GetTouch(0);
if (raycastManager.Raycast(touch.position, out var hits, TrackableType.PlaneWithinPolygon))
{
Pose hitPose = hits[0].pose;
Instantiate(objectPrefab, hitPose.position, hitPose.rotation);
}
}
}
}
```

Hardware & Performance Questions

What are the best AR/VR headsets for development?

Device	Platform	Best Use Case
Oculus Quest 2	Standalone / PC VR	General VR development, gaming
HTC Vive Pro	PC VR	High-end VR applications
Microsoft HoloLens	Mixed Reality	Enterprise AR applications
Magic Leap 2	AR/MR	Business & industrial AR
Meta Quest 3	Standalone MR	Mixed Reality applications

What is the ideal refresh rate for VR?

- **60 Hz:** Minimum viable for casual VR use.
- **90 Hz:** Standard for most VR headsets (Oculus Quest, HTC Vive).
- **120+ Hz:** Ideal for reducing motion sickness and achieving smooth visuals.

How do I optimize performance in AR & VR applications?

- **Use level-of-detail (LOD) models** to render fewer polygons at a distance.
- **Implement occlusion culling** to avoid rendering objects not visible to the user.
- **Use foveated rendering** to render only the area where the user is looking at full resolution.
- **Reduce draw calls** by combining multiple objects into a single mesh.

EXAMPLE: **Optimizing Object Rendering (Unity - C#)**

```
void Start()

{

QualitySettings.lodBias = 0.5f; // Reduce detail level for distant objects

}
```

Motion Sickness & Comfort

Why do some people feel motion sickness in VR?

MOTION SICKNESS IN VR occurs due to a **mismatch between visual input and inner ear balance perception.** Causes include:

- **Low frame rates** (below 90 FPS).
- **Rapid acceleration/deceleration.**
- **Camera movement without head tracking.**

How can I reduce VR motion sickness?

- **Increase frame rate** (target 90 FPS or higher).
- **Use teleportation-based movement** instead of continuous locomotion.
- **Reduce field of view (FoV) during motion.**
- **Enable VR comfort mode features** such as vignette effects.

EXAMPLE: **Implementing Teleportation in Unity VR (C#)**

```
using UnityEngine;

using UnityEngine.XR.Interaction.Toolkit;

public class VRTeleport : MonoBehaviour

{

public XRRayInteractor rayInteractor;
```

```
public XRInteractorLineVisual lineVisual;
void Update()
{
if (rayInteractor.TryGetCurrent3DRaycastHit(out RaycastHit hit))
{
transform.position = hit.point; // Teleport to targeted point
}
}
}
```

Monetization & Business Opportunities

How can AR & VR applications be monetized?

- **In-app purchases:** Sell virtual items, skins, or features.
- **Subscription models:** Charge for premium AR/VR content.
- **Advertising:** Implement AR ads in applications.
- **Enterprise solutions:** Offer AR/VR training, real estate visualization, and retail applications.

What industries benefit most from AR & VR?

Industry	Use Cases
Gaming & Entertainment	Immersive gaming, social VR experiences
Education	Virtual classrooms, interactive learning
Healthcare	VR therapy, medical training
Retail	AR try-ons, virtual showrooms
Real Estate	Virtual property tours
Manufacturing	AR-assisted assembly, remote maintenance

Future of AR & VR

What is the role of AR & VR in the Metaverse?

- **AR & VR are foundational technologies** for the Metaverse, allowing users to interact with digital worlds.
- **Decentralized virtual spaces** will enable cross-platform experiences.
- **Advancements in AI and blockchain** will enhance AR & VR interactions.

Conclusion

THIS FAQ SECTION PROVIDES answers to common AR & VR development questions, helping developers and businesses navigate the growing landscape of immersive technology. Whether you are a beginner exploring ARKit, an enterprise leveraging VR for training, or a developer optimizing graphics for performance, these insights serve as a foundation for AR & VR success.

www.ingramcontent.com/pod-product-compliance
Lightning Source LLC
LaVergne TN
LVHW090301210926
848480LV00001B/86
* 9 7 9 8 2 3 0 0 5 0 7 2 8 *